RESOURCE BOOKS FOR TEACHERS

series editor
ALAN MALEY

THE INTERNET

Scott Windeatt, David Hardisty, and David Eastment

OXFORD

OXFORD
UNIVERSITY PRESS

Great Clarendon Street, Oxford OX2 6DP

Oxford University Press is a department of the University
of Oxford. It furthers the University's objective of excellence
in research, scholarship, and education by publishing
worldwide in

Oxford New York

Athens Auckland Bangkok Bogotá Buenos Aires
Calcutta Cape Town Chennai Dar es Salaam Delhi
Florence Hong Kong Istanbul Karachi Kuala Lumpur
Madrid Melbourne Mexico City Mumbai Nairobi Paris
São Paulo Shanghai Singapore Taipei Tokyo Toronto Warsaw

with associated companies in Berlin Ibadan

Oxford and Oxford English are registered trade marks of
Oxford University Press in the UK and in certain other countries

ISBN 0-19-4372235

Typeset by Wyvern 21 Ltd., Bristol

Printed in China

Acknowledgements

The authors would like to thank the many colleagues who have given us inspiration for ideas in this book. We would also like to acknowledge the support of the British Council in Hong Kong in developing some of the material in the book. We should especially like to thank Martin Peacock and Rod Pryde for their support. We would also like to thank Tony Sibbons for his comments and Nina Blackett for her help in finalizing the manuscript.

Appendix B1, 'Surfing the Web', was based on a page produced by Charles Kelly which can be found at *http://www.aitech.ac.jp/~ckelly/*

There may be instances where we have been unable to trace or contact copyright holders before our printing deadline. The authors and publisher apologize for this apparent negligence. If notified, the publisher will be pleased to rectify any errors or omissions at the earliest opportunity.

To our children:
Christopher, Susan, Philip,
and Maria Ana

Contents

3 Focus on language skills

Foreword

The Internet was undeniably the most radical agent of change in the last quarter of the 20th century. It touches all our lives at many points, and its influence will continue to grow inexorably, and in probably unpredictable ways, in the 21st century. Language pedagogy cannot and should not be immune to the advantages the Internet offers—in information, in resources and in opportunities for global communication.

However, teachers' reactions to the Internet are typically emotion-driven. On the one hand there are those in whom it evokes anxiety and confusion. The response to 'infoglut' (the sheer quantity of information available), 'infosprawl' (the apparently chaotic manner in which it is organized) and to 'infobabble' (the triviality of so much of what is accessible) is at best a sort of mental block and at worst a passionate, Luddite resistance.

On the other hand there are those whose uncritically enthusiastic embracing of the Internet may produce equally negative results. A fascination with the technology at the expense of sound pedagogy can only be harmful, for all its superficial attractions.

The book provides a welcome corrective to both these emotional responses. The activities in Chapter 1 (Core Internet Skills) are specifically designed to lead both students and teachers through the skills of searching and saving on the Internet. They are clearly and unthreateningly presented, as well as providing interesting and productive language work. The chapter should build confidence even among technophobes.

The remaining two chapters (Focus on Language and Focus on Language Skills) offer a wide range of language-learning activities drawing on the resources of the Internet. The primary focus is always the language-learning payoff rather than the technical sophistication of the medium.

Features which will recommend themselves to novices and Net experts alike are the appendices and Website, which contain a wealth of information and links.

The book thus combines user-friendliness, pedagogically valuable activities, and state-of-the-art information. As such it will help teachers to use the Internet as a resource.

Alan Maley

The authors and series editor

Scott Windeatt teaches in the Language Centre at the University of Newcastle upon Tyne, where he is Director of the MA in Media Technology for TEFL. He has taught at secondary schools in the UK, and has worked in Finland, Romania, and Austria. Other countries he has visited to give lectures and workshops include Denmark, France, Germany, Indonesia, Italy, Japan, Malaysia, the Netherlands, the Philippines, Spain, and Qatar. His publications include books and articles on teaching grammar, computer-assisted language learning, computers and teacher training, computer-based language testing, classroom practice and observation, task-based learning, syllabus and materials design, and self-access learning. With David Hardisty, he wrote *CALL* (Computer-Assisted Language Learning) for this series in 1989.

David Hardisty teaches English to Media and Cultural Studies students at the Catholic University of Portugal and has also been a teacher and teacher trainer at The British Council in Lisbon since 1983. Before moving to Portugal he taught in the UK, Sudan, Spain, and Mexico. Other countries where he has given papers and workshops include the USA, Germany, Ireland, the Netherlands, and Spain. His publications include books and articles on computer-assisted language learning, general methodology, using the media, grammar teaching and learning, and using music in the classroom. With Scott Windeatt, he wrote *CALL* in this series.

David Eastment taught English in Japan and Italy before starting to specialize in the early 1980s in the application of computers to language learning. He worked for many years with the Bell Language Schools in Cambridge, where he was Director of Studies for Information Technology. He has run workshops and seminars in Europe, Asia, the Middle East, and South America, and has written and lectured extensively on the problems and the opportunities presented by the new technology. David now works as a freelance teacher, teacher trainer, and consultant. From 1994 to 1999 he was editor of *Issues*, the Newsletter of the International Association of Teachers of English as a Foreign Language (IATEFL), and he is a Fellow of the Royal Society for the Arts. He is the author of *The Internet and ELT*, a report for The British Council published by Summertown Publishing.

Alan Maley worked for The British Council from 1962 to 1988, serving as English Language Officer in Yugoslavia, Ghana, Italy, France, and China, and as Regional Representative in South India (Madras). From 1988 to 1993 he was Director-General of the Bell Educational Trust, Cambridge. From 1993 to 1998 he was Senior Fellow in the Department of English Language and Literature of the National University of Singapore. He is currently a freelance consultant and Director of the graduate programme at Assumption University, Bangkok. Among his publications are *Literature*, in this series, *Beyond Words*, *Sounds Interesting*, *Sounds Intriguing*, *Words*, *Variations on a Theme*, and *Drama Techniques in Language Learning* (all with Alan Duff), *The Mind's Eye* (with Françoise Grellet and Alan Duff), *Learning to Listen* and *Poem into Poem* (with Sandra Moulding), and *Short and Sweet*. He is also Series Editor for the Oxford Supplementary Skills series.

Introduction

Who is the book for?

This book is intended for language teachers who have at least some experience of working with computers, either for their personal use or for language teaching. However, since our Activities assume differing amounts of computer expertise, whether your computing experience is great or small, you will find ideas in the book that you can use.

The aims of the book

Although they have been used for teaching since the 1960s, computers only became practical and affordable for language learning in the early 1980s, when relatively inexpensive personal computers first became available. The first Computer-Assisted Language Learning (**CALL**) programs were mainly used for manipulating words and sentences, playing games with students, testing them, and giving them feedback on their performance. Used in this way the computer has often been described as the 'medium of the second chance' (because the activities usually let you try more than once to get an answer right) and of risk-taking (because you can make mistakes in your answers without other students knowing). We feel that both descriptions can be applied to activities on the **Internet**.

As computers became more powerful, and multimedia software became practical, the early 1990s saw the emergence of CD-ROMs, storing complete encyclopaedias or language courses with text, graphics, and audio or video. Commercial products of this sort, which are professionally produced, reliable, and straightforward to use, have a place in many classrooms.

In many ways, however, the challenges presented to both students and teachers by the Internet can provide a more interesting, rewarding experience. The Net is a huge, rich resource, much of it as yet unmapped. Even finding useful information requires skill and judgement. The variety of resources is so great that deciding how to exploit resources once you find them can be a challenge in itself. And what of the millions of Net users, connected into a vast communications network? How do you contact them? How can you ensure that your students' Internet time is productive in terms of language learning? What sort of language-learning activities is the Internet best used for?

This book will help to answer these and other questions by presenting ideas for computer-based language-learning activities using the Internet and the **World Wide Web**. We feel that the main distinguishing feature of the Internet, which sets it apart from more traditional types of CALL, is that it is a medium of exploration. In our Activities, we try to encourage both you and your students to explore for yourselves the huge potential of this medium, not only as a source of practice texts, but as a way of releasing creativity and imagination, both yours and theirs. Our Activities all have the aim of providing language practice, or of helping students to learn new language, but they also have the additional aim of helping you and your students acquire the skills that you need to make the best use of the Internet in learning or practising language. We would like you to think of this book as a starting point.

Why use the Internet for language learning?

The Internet is beginning to transform language learning, first of all by making available to teachers and students an enormous range of information and resources. Information, on virtually any subject, and resources, including articles, stories, poems, books, video and audio clips, music, and millions of images, are all only a few mouse clicks away—as long as you know how to find them.

As a means of communication, the Internet allows students around the world to interact with one another cheaply, quickly, and reliably, opening up the classroom to the real world in a way which has never before been possible.

Because the Internet is such a powerful tool for information and communication, there can be much more integration of computer work into the language curriculum. Both teachers and students can start to use the Internet as a source of material for learning and teaching in the same way as they currently use books, magazines, newspapers, television, audio, and video. Eventually, they will probably use more Internet-based than print resources, simply because these will be more easily available. Access to the Internet will, in fact, lead to a change in the way languages are learnt. Not only does the Internet provide a faster and more convenient alternative to conventional communicative writing, but it is beginning to allow audio and video communication in ways that have never before been practical.

The Internet will also lead to more cross-curricular work. Skills needed to use the Internet for language learning will be similar to those needed in other subjects in the curriculum, while Internet resources found in the language classroom will often be relevant to other subjects. Students may find that the information they need for other subjects is only available in English, so that they may be able to practise their language skills at the same time as studying other subjects.

It is often claimed that computers are worth using in the language classroom for their potential to motivate. In our experience, students generally enjoy using computers, but the motivation generated simply by the novelty of a 'new' medium is likely to be short-lived, unless the students feel some benefit from their tasks. Our Activities, therefore, all have a language-learning purpose, and are never designed purely to 'display the technology'.

Censorship

Because there is very little censorship on the Web, it is possible to come across pages that you object to, or whose content you would rather your students did not see. It is possible to use software that will tackle this problem to some extent. There are programs that allow you to specify particular sites that students are not allowed access to. It is possible as well for such software to exclude pages that contain particular words so that, in theory, you can deny your students access to pages dealing with particular topics.

There are a number of such programs which can either be bought, or which are available on particular Websites. However, there are at least three questions worth considering if you are thinking of using such software:

1 How well does the software work? Software for excluding particular Websites is likely to work quite adequately, but more general censoring or filtering of Web pages, especially by specifying particular words or phrases, is likely to work in a fairly crude fashion, and may well exclude quite unobjectionable pages. The software works rather like a grammar and style checker in a word-processor. How useful do you find that software?

2 How serious is the problem of unsuitable content? How often do you come across unsuitable content yourself, or how often do you find your students looking at content you consider unsuitable? If this is not really a problem at present, maybe it is not worth worrying about.

3 Should you censor your students' reading? If there is unsuitable content available on the Web, then rather than prevent access to it, perhaps teachers should help students develop the critical skills and the responsibility they need to deal with it.

Appendix D3, page 119, gives examples of Websites from which you can download software to control access to the Web and particular sites.

How you can use the Internet for language learning

The Internet is a tool which has great potential in the language classroom, but its effectiveness in practice depends to a large extent on the way it is exploited by teacher and students. Your general methodology is also important. This section will consider some methodological issues which relate both to the Internet and to language teaching.

Hardware: how to arrange the computer room

If sufficient equipment is available, lessons may involve students working individually at computers, but most classes will also involve some pair and group work at the computers, as well as pair, group, or whole-class work away from the computers.

The optimum situation for most activities is a large classroom with at least one computer for every two or three students. Ideally, the computers will be located around the walls, or in clusters, with plenty of desk space and room to move around.

Many teachers will find, however, that computer rooms have been set up with subjects other than English in mind. Computers will often be found in rows, with little room between them, so it will be difficult for students to move around and for teachers to move from student to student or from group to group. In rooms like this, it is usually not possible to re-arrange furniture, but remember that much of the preparation and follow-up involved in a good Internet lesson can be done perfectly well away from the computers.

Learner training

The great advantage of the Internet over earlier CALL is the fact that it is not necessary to learn how to use a large number of programs. The Internet can be used effectively with only two pieces of software—a **browser** to allow access to the pages of the Web, and an **email** program. Of course, there is plenty of other software available, and you or your students might want to learn how to use additional software for purposes such as

conferencing, creating Web pages, or manipulating graphics. But for most purposes—and for 90 per cent of the activities in this book—a browser and an email program are all that is required.

The amount of technical training students need will vary from institution to institution. Computers might be set up in such a way that students only need to be able to switch on the computer and click on an icon; or they might need to specify a certain **server** and log in with a password before they can get started. What is important is to have a clear idea of what skills students will need to get connected and to carry out tasks on the Internet. Teachers often *assume* that their students have these skills, but it is vital to be sure that this is in fact the case.

A useful tool in many situations is a checklist of tightly specified competencies which the student is asked either to tick or perhaps to demonstrate in practice. A sample checklist might read:

I can:

Start a browser ....

Type in a URL ....

Scroll around a page ....

Identify a graphic ....

Find a word in a long Web page ....

Open a new window in the browser ....

etc. ....

In addition to the purely technical skills, students are also likely to need formal training in study skills. They will need to be able to keep a record of what they have done, for example, and to keep a notebook (whether electronic or on paper) for recording new vocabulary and structures they encounter.

Lesson management

Most of the activities in this book contain stages before and after the students use the Internet and, depending on the computer resources of your teaching institution, these may have to be done outside the computer room. Once students begin working on the computers, however, what many teachers find pleasing is that, unless they need help, the attention of students is away from the teacher. This allows you more flexibility in managing the lesson, and in particular there is often more time to work with individuals and groups than in an ordinary class.

Material from the Internet can be used with a variety of levels by allowing students themselves to choose the kind of material they work with, and by varying the kind of task they are asked to perform. For example, if students have to visit newspaper sites in order to produce their own newspaper, they can be given a choice of Websites, of the kind of news they select, and of the task they are to carry out with the news they find.

Pre-computer work

In some cases, before beginning an activity on the computer, it will be necessary to pre-teach vocabulary, or a specific function or structure. In every case, however, you will need to ensure that the students know exactly what they have to do when they begin work on the computers. Demonstrations are invaluable, and work a good deal better if the whole class can look comfortably at a large display, rather than cluster around a computer screen. Several solutions are possible, including overhead display panels, 'beamers' (like a cinema projector), a machine with a very large monitor, or software which allows you to control what appears on the students' screens.

If no projection device or software is available, think about alternative ways in which the class can be prepared for the task. Example printouts from sites to be visited are one possibility. Another is to demonstrate the task to representatives from each of the groups while the rest of the class reads instructions for the task. The representatives can then return to their groups to demonstrate the task. Clear sets of printed instructions are important, with or without a demonstration. Above all, whatever technique you adopt, it is worth preparing the students carefully as there will be fewer calls for help from them when they are working at the computers.

Computer work

Try to resist the temptation to interfere while students are actually working at the computer. Only intervene if you are specifically asked for help. If the activity has been well prepared, and the students suitably trained, this is likely to be infrequent. Instead, use the time to monitor what the students are saying to each other, and how they are going about their task.

Post-computer work

It is important that anything done in the computer room should be transferable back to the normal classroom, and any Internet activity should be planned from the outset with some kind of follow-up activity in mind. The Activities in this book give an indication of the wide range of follow-up tasks that can be carried out.

Wherever possible, students should have something physical that they can take away with them from the computer room, so that they have a record of what they have done for follow-up work or for end-of-course revision. This might take the form of a completed worksheet, or a printout of a Web page, or something they themselves have created. They should at least take a copy of their work away with them on a disk. If you are planning to print, make sure that you don't leave it until the end of the session, especially if you only have one slow printer!

Students working at computers

Students can work individually if sufficient computers are available, but even with one computer for each student it can be useful to work in groups, especially for tasks such as problem-solving activities which require an exchange of opinions. However, as with any classroom activity, it is important to remember that the task itself and your overall approach will influence the way the students work. Simply putting students in groups does not guarantee that useful discussion will take place, and just putting students together in front of a computer connected to the Internet will not automatically ensure useful interaction within the groups.

 When several groups are working within a class, it is possible to use a variety of interaction patterns. Groups can communicate with each other in person, by sending each other emails, by placing material produced during the class on a public drive on the network, or by re-forming into new groups. This allows for a variety of forms of information transfer.

Note that if students wish to produce, save or share material, it is important to make sure that these activities will be possible on the network you are planning to use. Many institutions do not allow students to save work on the network and do not provide shared drives where students can save materials for other students to look at (if this is the case in your institution, try and persuade the people responsible that there are useful learning benefits to be gained from providing space on shared public drives).

Working with small numbers of computers

Computers do not have to be located in a special 'laboratory'. It is often more convenient to keep them all together but, provided that the school is networked, there is no reason why computers cannot be grouped in twos and threes in various areas of the building, or indeed why they cannot be put into individual classrooms. In well-resourced institutions, it is increasingly common to find not only a cassette-player and video in each classroom, but a PC too, which can then be used as a normal, workaday tool, and a permanent classroom resource.

If some kind of projection device is available, the single computer can be used as a large electronic board for the whole class to look at, to watch 'breaking news', for example, or to display input for a non-computer language activity. If projection is not available, then 'lockstep' teaching (in which all the students in the class are doing the same thing) is not possible and classes need to be organized in a different way. Students can work individually, in pairs, or in groups, on, for example, project-work. One group might be preparing a questionnaire, another might be planning their project, another might be watching a video or looking up material in an encyclopaedia, and another might be working on the Web.

Using the computer for self-study

If computers are available in libraries or self-access centres, or if students have their own computers and access to the Internet, self-study activities should be built into the syllabus. These can take the form of preparatory or follow-up activities for a class, or individual or group projects. Alternatively, some of the activities carried out in class time can be repeated by students in their own time (for example, if they enjoy using the vocabulary quizzes and puzzles in Activity 2.2 on page 52, they might want to do more themselves outside class). The computers can also be used for searching the Internet for material that students can use in their homework, and for sending and receiving emails to other students or to you.

However, simply placing one or more Internet-connected computers in the self-access centre achieves nothing unless students are helped to plan their use of it. The student might otherwise just as well use a computer in a cybercafé or his or her own bedroom. Some schools provide self-study pathways, often on laminated cards, for students to follow, and group together Web 'bookmarks' for specific learning tasks. Such materials, which can be organized by level, language skill, or topic, tend to be both popular and useful, but are time-consuming to create and maintain.

Integration into the curriculum

The Internet can be used throughout a language course and not just for a few lessons which focus on computer work. For example, extra data for language points which are dealt with in the normal classroom lessons can be found by searching on the Web and analysed in class, as in Activity 1.1 on page 24.

For students who are also studying other subjects, there are a number of additional language-learning possibilities. If they consult the Internet for information on other subjects, much of the information they will find is likely to be in English. Language teachers may find that they are asked, by the students or by other teachers, to provide language support for other subjects.

Are there any 'rules' for using the Internet for language teaching?

The most important point to make about using the Internet for language teaching is that you should rely on your experience as a teacher in planning and using the Internet with your learners. However, there are a number of 'tips' that we have found useful:

1 Be prepared

As with all activities in the classroom, it is worth preparing as carefully as you have time for, and this is especially true when you are using the Internet. It is worth checking out Web pages before a lesson even if you have used them before, as they may have changed. It is also worth having some alternative activities available in case technical problems mean you have to adapt your lesson.

2 Be patient

There are times when the Web can run very slowly, or you are unable to access a particular Website. If this happens when you are looking for resources for a lesson, try postponing the search until later—you will probably find there are times when the Web runs more quickly, and inaccessible Web sites suddenly re-appear.

3 Be organized

It is easy to skim through lots of Web pages and forget where they are when you want to find them again. Get into the habit of keeping a record of pages you visit which you think might be useful in future, and train your students to do this as well (you can use **Bookmarks** and **Favorites** for this).

4 Be exploratory

The Internet is constantly developing and presents many possibilities for language learning that have hardly been explored. Use your imagination, try things out, and take the occasional risk!

5 Be critical

The Web is a place where more or less anyone can publish more or less what they want. Whilst this means that information is available on a vast amount of subjects, it also means you should look critically at any information you find there, and help your students develop a critical approach.

6 Be co-operative

So many resources are available on the Web that you will never be able to discover all of the useful ones yourself. Agree with other teachers and with your students to share information about useful Web pages that you find (see Activities 1.5–1.8).

7 Be realistic

The Internet is a tool or a resource and will only be useful if you understand its strengths and weaknesses. A saying we used in our previous book *CALL* applies equally well to using the Internet: 'Any teacher who can be replaced by a computer should be.' (Anon)

How to use this book

What you need in order to use this book

What equipment you need

Each Activity lists the equipment and the software which are
required, but the following general points are important:

1 Computers: number

You need at least one computer! Some Activities can be done with
just one computer; most require one computer per group of
students. However, most of the Activities can be adapted to suit
different numbers of machines.

2 Computers: type

You can do virtually all of the Activities on any type of computer.
In other words, it doesn't matter whether you have PCs, Macs, or
other kinds of computer—if you can run a Web **browser** and
access the Internet, you should still be able to do the Activities, or
adapt them so that you can do them.

3 Multimedia

Some Activities assume that you have at least one computer with a
sound-card and speakers.

4 The Internet

All of the Activities involve email, the Web, or both, and assume
that you have a connection to the Internet on at least one machine.
This may be via a modem attached to a particular machine, or via
a local network which has a connection to the Internet. If your
Internet connection is not on a classroom machine, you may be
able to adapt the Activities by saving Internet materials to disk, or
by distributing printed copies to students.

5 Software

The Activities are based on software that is generally available, and
is not machine-specific (i.e. it is likely to be available in some form
on PCs, Macs, and so on). The main types of software used are:

- Web browsers and plugins
- word-processors
- email facilities
- newsgroup facilities
- 'chat' software
- Web-authoring software

See Appendix D3, page 119, for sources of some of this software on the Web.

What you need to know

The book does not assume that you are an expert computer user, but it does assume that you know how to start up a computer, or log on to a networked computer, and how to start programs running. To make the most of the book, you should also have some experience of using word-processing software and, for some activities, of using email and the Web. This book is not a manual for teaching you how to use computers; if you have no experience at all of using computers, you will need the help of a more experienced colleague. See also the Bibliography on page 132 for books which give more technical advice.

How this book is organized

The book is divided into three chapters, each of which contains Activities showing how computers can be used to practise a particular aspect of language. Each chapter has a different emphasis.

Chapter 1 presents Activities that practise some of the 'core Internet skills' of searching and storing, evaluating, and communicating that will help you make the best use of the Internet for language learning. Chapter 2 contains examples of Activities that focus on vocabulary and grammar, while Chapter 3 consists of Activities that practise reading, writing, listening, speaking, translating, and integrated skills.

There are also a number of appendices, including a glossary of Internet terms. Words in the book which are explained in the glossary are in **bold** the first time you meet them. Other appendices provide useful information such as contact addresses, bibliographies, Web links suggested for each activity, and advice about various aspects of using computers for language learning.

How each Activity is organized

For each Activity we provide the following information:

Level	the level of student for which the Activity is most likely to be suitable;
Time	a rough guide to the time the Activity is likely to take;
Aims	the purpose of the Activity;
Technical requirements	the equipment and software you need for the Activity, and any special knowledge you and your students need to do the Activity;
Knowledge	any special knowledge you and your students need to do the Activity;
Preparation	what you have to do or prepare before the Activity;
Procedure	step-by-step instructions for each Activity, including work away from the computer;
Follow-up	suggestions for follow-up work, either in class, or for self-access, or homework;
Variations	we sometimes describe ways in which you can modify the Activity for different levels of student, for different numbers of computers, or to exploit different types of material;
Notes	we often add comments that we think you will find useful when doing the Activity.

Most activities also have their own entry in the Appendix E, Activity Links (page 121) and a corresponding, regularly updated entry on the book's Website which is in the Oxford University Press pages at:

http://www.oup.com/elt/rbt.internet

The Web is a dynamic medium, and Websites are constantly changing, moving, or disappearing. We recommend that you look at our Website to check that the sites listed in Appendix E are still available and suitable. Inclusion in the list does not mean that a site is endorsed by the authors or publishers of this book. Always check out sites before using them in class.

Our Website also includes several worksheets, which you can download and adapt to suit your classes, as well as updated technical data. Readers are also invited to email us their ideas and feedback; we will publish good ideas in our regular updates of the Website.

How you can use the book

The best way to use the book is to dip into it, as most of the Activities can be adapted for different circumstances. However, if you don't have much experience of using computers or of using the Internet, you should work through Chapter 1 first. In each chapter users will find there is some progression in difficulty in the Activities within each section.

1 Core Internet skills

Introduction

There are a number of core enabling skills which are important for helping language teachers and students make the most effective use of the Internet and the World Wide Web. They include knowing how to:

- search for information or materials;
- sort and store the results of your search;
- evaluate what you have found;
- use the Internet to communicate with other users.

This chapter gives further explanation of each of these skills, and provides examples of Activities that you can use to develop your own and your students' expertise in them.

Searching and sorting

Why do we need to learn how to search?

The Web is an enormously useful collection of information and materials, rather like a huge, sprawling library. Unlike a library, however, material on the Web is not carefully organized and stored, and you will need to use one of the tools that have been designed to help you find what you want. It is essential that teachers and students develop the skills and strategies that will allow them to use these tools effectively.

Searching terminology

When you carry out a search, you use a **search engine**. This is a program that asks you to type a word or words, or choose from a menu; the program will then carry out a search, which works in a similar way to the 'Find' function in word-processors. Search engines can be found at well-known sites like AltaVista, Lycos, Hotbot, and Yahoo!, but there are many others, and new ones appear regularly.

The search engine will search for pages containing the word or words you have asked it to search for. The pages it finds are known as 'hits', so if it finds 15 pages, it might report those as 15 hits.

The pages or hits will have an address, which is where the page is located on the Web. The address is known as a **URL** (a **u**niform **r**esource **l**ocator) and will look something like this:

> *http://www.oup.com/*

If you want to keep a note of an address, in case you might want to revisit the page in future, you can place it in the Bookmarks or Favorites folder of your Web **browser** (the program you use to read information on the Web).

Searching on the Web

What you want when searching is to get the widest possible coverage with the greatest degree of relevance (i.e. find as much information as possible, but only find the kind of information you want), so it is important to develop effective Web-searching strategies to achieve this.

Web-searching strategies

Decide if the information is likely to be available on the Web

The Web contains a vast amount of information, but it is important to realize that it may still not contain the information you want. A great deal of time can be wasted searching in vain for information that is simply not available on the Web.

Decide if the information is available more conveniently somewhere else

The information may be available on the Web, but it may be quicker and easier to ask someone who already knows the answer, or to consult a book—a dictionary, for example—rather than search on the Web.

Decide which 'search engine' to use

There are many different search engines currently available. New ones appear regularly, and existing ones develop and change. What is important, however, is to remember that the same search on two different search engines will usually give quite different results, so:

- if a search using one search engine doesn't give you the results you want, try another one;

- don't just use the same search engine all the time—try others you haven't used before;
- from time to time go back to a search engine you have stopped using, as it may have changed.

Searching techniques

There are a number of different approaches to searching that can be taken. Not all approaches are available in all search engines, and different search engines can be better for one kind of search than another. You should experiment with the range of possibilities for searching that each search engine offers.

Basic searches

These are the easiest, so try them first.

Search in categorized information

Information is sometimes pre-organized into categories (such as 'Entertainment', 'Education', 'Technology'), and looking in these categories and their sub-categories ('Entertainment: Movies: Actors') can find the information you want quickly and easily.

Search using the exact word

If the information is not already organized into categories, typing in the exact word to find the information you are searching for is the simplest. This is how you would usually search for information.

Search using an alternative word

If the first word you search for doesn't find the information you want, first of all check your spelling. If that is correct (don't forget differences between British and American English spelling), you could try an alternative word, such as a synonym.

Search using 'natural language'

Some search engines allow you to type in a statement or a question and they will try to identify the information you want.

Advanced searches

Your search may give you very many 'hits'. If the information you
want isn't in the first few 'hits' (for example, on the first page or
two), try one of these more advanced searches.

Search using a wildcard

Another way of widening your search is to use a 'wildcard'. *search*
will find just *search*. *search★* will find *search, searches, searched,
searching, searcher,* and so on. *★search* will find *search, research,* etc.
Note that search engines vary in their treatment of wildcards; for
example, some will not allow wildcards at the beginning of a word.

Words plus categories

With some search engines you can use a combination of words and
categories. For example, you can search for a Web page about a
particular actor, in a particular film, and ask only for pages that
also have a picture. Some search engines will allow you to search
using words that you type in, plus categories that you specify (for
example, you may be able to specify pages with pictures by
choosing that as a category rather than having to type it).

And, or, not (Boolean) searches

More complicated searches can sometimes be carried out using
AND, OR, or NOT (or + or −). There is a detailed example in
Appendix B3 ('Searching for information on the Web', page 107).

Storing the results of searches

Keeping an accurate record of material that you have consulted is
a key study skill that all students need to develop. This is
important whatever medium you are working in, but it is especially
important when working with the Web as it is very easy to skim
through a great many Web pages while forgetting to note which
ones you have looked at. Records for paper-based material are
likely to be kept as written references in notes or on cards, but
records of Web pages can be stored on the computer as
Bookmarks or **Favorites**.

Saving URLs

If you visit a Web page that you think you will want to visit again,
you can save a copy of the address (the URL) as a Bookmark in
Netscape Navigator, and as a Favorite in Microsoft **Internet
Explorer**. Storing Web page addresses not only saves you having

to remember an address and type it in again (and URLs aren't really designed to be easy to remember or to type), but they can also be used as a record of work that has been done. Students can save Web page addresses that they have visited to gather information for a project, for example, or they can save the addresses of Web pages that they may not need at the moment, but which might be useful in future.

Organizing URLs

The Web page addresses students save will be most useful if they are categorized rather than just left as one long list. In Web browsers, different categories of information can be organized and saved in different folders. Students can save the addresses of Web pages they have visited in a particular lesson in a separate folder for that lesson. It is then easy for them to show those pages to the rest of the class, or to you, as a record of the work they have done, or of the pages they found interesting or useful. Research for project work can also be saved as Web page addresses in a dedicated folder. Students can also set up folders on topics such as their hobbies, or language topics such as vocabulary and grammar. They can then build up collections of Web page addresses on these topics over time.

Backing up Bookmarks and Favorites

Any information that is stored on a computer should be copied regularly so that a backup is available in case something happens to the original. This is just as true of Bookmarks and Favorites as of any other computer data.

Bookmarks in Netscape are held in a file called Bookmarks.htm, which can be copied to another directory or disk like any other file. A copy of the Bookmarks.htm file can also be saved using 'Save as' under the 'Edit bookmarks' option. In Explorer, the Favorites are held in a sub-directory called Favorites, and the whole sub-directory can be copied and saved.

Web 'history'

Even if you don't save the address of a Web page as a bookmark, Netscape and Explorer will record the pages you visit. You can look at this record by choosing the History option in both browsers. This feature can be extremely useful, especially if you forget to save the address of a page you later decide to revisit. However, it is not a substitute for keeping Bookmarks or Favorites, as History addresses cannot be organized, and will eventually be deleted.

1.1 It all depends

LEVEL	**Intermediate and above**
TIME	**15–30 minutes**
AIMS	**To practise searching for text on the Web; to demonstrate the use of Web searching to check grammatical features; to revise prepositions used with 'depend'.**
TECHNICAL REQUIREMENTS	One computer per student, or per group of 2–3 students, with an Internet connection and a Web **browser**.

PREPARATION

1 If you have not used the AltaVista search engine before, familiarize yourself with the site and the way it works. Its **URL** is in Appendix E, page 121 (see Notes).

2 Prepare a list of grammatical items for the students to search for. Try out the searches before the class. Copy the worksheet below for your students, or prepare one of your own.

PROCEDURE

1 Give the students a short gap-filling activity such as the one on the next page and ask them to complete it.

2 When they have finished the gap-filling Activity, students should draw a table like the one on the next page.

3 Send students to the AltaVista search engine site.

4 In the Search box, they should type the phrase *"depend of"* (see notes below) and click on Search. Tell them to make a note in the table of the number of 'hits' they find.

5 Students should copy some of the sentences containing *depend of* and paste them into a word-processor document. They might have to open the links to the pages where *depend of* occurs to copy these sentences.

6 They should follow the same procedure with *depend from* and *depend on*.

7 Ask the students to compare the number of 'hits' for each of the expressions, and to compare their results with those obtained by the other students.

8 Ask them to think about what the results mean. The fact that *depend on* is found so much more frequently than the other expressions suggests that it is likely to be the expression they should use.

9 Ask the students to look at some of the examples of the different expressions. *Depend from* appears to be found in some legal contexts, or in technical documents, where it means 'to hang from'. *Depend of* is often found in examples like '… *depend, of course, on* …'.

Which of these words can go in the gaps in the examples below?
on, of, from

It would depend .... what version.

Depend .... the alliance.

Our clients depend .... us.

I don't depend .... you.

Cancer research: Because lives depend .... it.

	Number of examples	The sentence the phrase is in, and the address where it was found
Depend of		
Depend from		
Depend on		

Photocopiable © Oxford University Press

VARIATIONS

Examples of other searches that can provide interesting results include:

Different to:　39925 examples

Different from:　483059 examples

Different than:　138434 examples

Wicked	Conventional dictionaries are unlikely to have examples of the most recent slang usage, such as *wicked* (meaning *very good*).

NOTES

1 We usually suggest a choice of search engines, but at the time of going to press this activity only works using AltaVista. See our Website *http://www.oup.com/elt/rbt.internet* for regular updates.

2 To search for a whole phrase, rather than the individual words within that phrase, some search engines require that the phrase be included in quotation marks, i.e. "depend on". Others require that a + sign be placed between the words, i.e. depend+on. If in doubt, check in the Help of the search engine. See also Appendix B3 (page 107) for more information.

3 Once students have understood how to use a search facility to verify language points, this activity can be carried out regularly. Classes can make notes of language points which come up, and different groups can be given the task of finding out information about them. This can of course be done by groups on just one computer, either in the educational institution or even at home.

1.2 Desperately seeking . . .

LEVEL

All

TIME

15–30 minutes

AIMS

To practise scanning and interpreting the results of a Web search.

TECHNICAL REQUIREMENTS

One computer per student, or per group of 2–3 students, with an Internet connection and a Web browser.

PREPARATION

1 Choose a search engine to use in the lesson. You will find some suggestions in Appendix E ('Activity links', page 121) or on our Website at *http://www.oup.com/elt/rbt.internet*

For hints on searching the Web, see 1.1 or Appendix B3 (page 107).

2 Before the class, run a search using the name of a pop star that will interest your students. Depending on the types of hits returned, prepare a worksheet, or copy the one supplied, or download it from our Website and adapt it. This should be printed out, or distributed electronically to the students.

At which sites are you most likely to find:	Sites	Why?	Results
. . . pictures of Madonna?			
. . . sound-files of Madonna's songs?			
. . . the price of Madonna's CDs?			
. . . information about concerts Madonna will be appearing at?			
. . . video clips of Madonna?			
. . . an interview with Madonna?			
. . . where Madonna's records are in the charts?			
. . . the most recent information about Madonna?			
. . . 'official' information about Madonna?			
. . . the words of Madonna's songs?			
. . . nothing about Madonna at all?			

Photocopiable © Oxford University Press

PROCEDURE

1 Tell the students that they are going to identify which sites are most likely to contain particular kinds of information about a pop singer.

2 Send the students to the search engine, and tell them the name they should search for. Ask them to answer the questions on the worksheet about the sites in the resulting hit list, and to complete the *'Sites'* and *'Why?'* columns. They should not go to the sites yet.

Here is an example of a search done using Hotbot:

At which of the following sites are you most likely to find:	Web sites	Why?	Results
… pictures of Madonna?	http://www. madonnafanclub.com/	This is the official fan club	
… sound-files of Madonna's songs?	http://www.dotmusic.com/ http://www.hofstra.edu/~v maffea1/madonna.html	Includes real audio clips, dance,video, live coverage Includes real audio clips The Music Archive	
… the price of Madonna's CDs?	http://www.dotmusic.com/ http://www.cdnow.com/ switch/from=sr934564/tar get=buyweb_purchase/ddcn =MSI-	Shop, CDs Sale Up to 30% off through Aug.10	
… information about concerts Madonna will be appearing at?	http://www.tv.com/ Webcast/101996.html	Madonna tickets and tour schedules	
…video clips of Madonna?	http://www.hofstra.edu/~v maffea1/madonna.html	The Music Archive: Madonna soundclips	
… an interview with Madonna?	http://letterman.iscool.com /madonna http://www.mrshowbiz.com/ archive/news/Todays_Sto ries/961209/12_9_96_1 madonna.html	Madonna on the Late Show with David Letterman.... includes pictures and classic audio clips of her. Oprah Lands Madonna Interview	
… where Madonna's records are in the charts?	http://www.dotmusic.com/	latest official UK charts	
… the most recent information about Madonna?	Http://www.dotmusic.com/	latest music news	
… 'official' information about Madonna?	http://www.madonnafanclub. com/	Official Madonna Fan Club	
… the words of Madonna's songs?	http://gene.wins.uva.nl/~bo nsee/lyrics/madonna_1.html	Madonna - Don't Cry For Me Argentina. The newest lyrics from the music charts	
… nothing about Madonna at all?	http://www.madonnainn. com/	Madonna Inn - San Luis Obispo, California – A hotel!	

3 Discuss the students' answers.

4 Tell students to check their answers by going to the sites.

5 Discuss the results they got when checking their answers. Were their guesses right or wrong? Was the information at the sites what they expected? What have they learnt that would help them choose from lists like this in future?

1.3 Starspotting

LEVEL

All

TIME

30 minutes

AIMS

To practise refining a Web search to find exactly the information you want; to compare different search engines and Web directories; to find material that could be used for project work.

TECHNICAL REQUIREMENTS

One computer per student, or per group of 2–3 students, with an Internet connection and a Web browser.

PREPARATION

1 Choose a film star who will appeal to your students. Do some Web searches to check that there are a large number of resources about the star on the Web. Practise the activity searches before the class.

2 Prepare a worksheet for your students, or use the one shown here.

PROCEDURE

1 Tell the students that they are going to search the Web for references to a movie actor or actress. The aim is to find a picture of the actor or actress in a particular film—in this case a picture of Ewan McGregor in *Star Wars Episode 1*.

2 Ask the students how many references they think they might find to Ewan McGregor on the Web. Then ask them how many they think they might find to *Star Wars*.

3 The number of references to either is likely to be very large and not very manageable; students would not have time to check them all out. Ask them how they think they can do a search to find the smallest number of references.

4 Put them into pairs or small groups and give half of the groups *Search Worksheet 1* and the other half *Search Worksheet 2*.

5 Tell the students who have *Search Worksheet 1* to go to the search engine you have chosen and follow the instructions on it.

6 Tell the students with *Search Worksheet 2* to go to the Web directory you have chosen. Remind them not to use the Search box, but to choose appropriate categories until they find references to a picture of *Ewan McGregor* in *Star Wars*.

Search Worksheet 1: AltaVista

Instructions
Go to the AltaVista search engine.
Search for *mcgregor* and note down the number of 'hits' in the grid below.
Search for *"ewan mcgregor"*.
Then search for *"star wars"*.
Then search for +*"ewan mcgregor"*+*"star wars"*.
Finally search for +*"ewan mcgregor"*+*"star wars"*+*image:ewan*.
Remember to note the number of hits in the grid below.
Tell the teacher when you have finished.
Check the sites you find at the end of your search to make sure you have found what you want.

Search words	Number of 'hits'
mcgregor	
"ewan mcgregor"	
"star wars"	
+"ewan mcgregor"+"star wars"	
+"ewan mcgregor"+"star wars" +image:ewan	

7   Remind both groups that at each stage they should note the number of hits they find. They should check the sites they find at the end of their search to make sure they have found the picture they want.

8   When the groups have found a suitable site, they should tell you. Check their pages and note which of the searches was quickest.

9   Discuss the results of refining the search and the number of hits found for each search.

10   Discuss the possible drawbacks of refining and narrowing down the search too much. For example, it is possible that you will exclude some useful references by narrowing the search down too much.

Search Worksheet 2: Yahoo!

Instructions	
Go to the Yahoo! Web directory	
Do not use the Search box. Choose appropriate categories until you find references to a picture of *Ewan McGregor* in *Star Wars*.	
Make a note of the categories you choose in the grid below.	
Make a note of the number of 'hits' you find, in the grid.	
Tell the teacher when you have finished.	
Check the sites you find to make sure you have found the picture you want.	
Search categories	*Number of 'hits'*
Entertainment [Xtra!] Cool Links, Movies, Music, Humor . . .	

Photocopiable © Oxford University Press

11 Discuss the differences between the searches using the search engine and the directory. How long did the searches take? Was it easier to specify search words or to choose categories? Were the results the same? Were the results better from the search engine or from the directory? Which one would the students use for future searches? Why?

NOTES

This activity familiarizes the students with different types of search engines and Web directories. It is important for them to realize that different search engines and directories will give different results.

1.4 Where did I put it?

LEVEL	**Elementary and above**
TIME	**30–45 minutes**
AIMS	**To practise classifying and grouping Web browser Bookmarks or Favorites.**
TECHNICAL REQUIREMENTS	One computer per group of 2–3 students, with an Internet connection and a Web browser.
KNOWLEDGE	You need to know how to create a Bookmarks or Favorites folder (see pages 22–3).
PREPARATION	Prepare a Bookmark or Favorites file consisting of about 20 sites of different types, which could be classified in different ways. Ideas for suitable sites can be found in Appendix E ('Activity links', page 121) or on our Website at *http://www.oup.com/elt/rbt.internet*

PROCEDURE

1 Ask students which three Websites they visit most often. Ask them to give a category name to their sites, for example, 'Music', 'Movies', or 'News'.

2 Check they understand how to 'bookmark' favourite locations.

3 Put the students into groups of 2–3 at each computer and tell them to load the Bookmarks or Favorites file you have created.

4 Tell the students to look at the various sites to check what information they offer.

5 They should then discuss and agree on how to group the sites into four main categories.

6 Students should compare the categories they have chosen.

VARIATION 1

The choice of sites depends on students. Teenagers can be given sites which relate to their own interests; undergraduates can be given sites which relate to various aspects of their area of study. If possible, try and choose sites which allow more than one classification system.

VARIATION 2

The students will need to learn how to make folders in the Bookmarks or Favorites file and place the sites in the appropriate folders. This could be done at the end of this Activity, or in a later lesson.

VARIATION 3

At a later stage, students who have a lot of bookmarks of their own could compare their criteria for organizing them. Students could also discuss how they organize their own files for programs such as word-processing or information saved from the Internet.

1 An Internet browser allows you to make a record of favourite sites on the Internet by 'bookmarking' them. Once students start using the Internet regularly, they can very quickly create a very large list of favourite locations. This activity helps them to organize these sites.

2 If you do this lesson with more than one class, make a safety copy of the bookmark file each time so that you do not have to spend time restoring it to its original form.

Evaluating

Most computer software is published in the same way as materials in conventional media, so that you have information such as the name of the publisher, and perhaps the name of the author, which can help you to judge what you are reading, buying, or using. However, this is not usually the case with content on the Web. There is very little policing or censorship of the Internet and information can be placed on the Web by almost anyone for almost any purpose. It is therefore especially important to think carefully about the status of information on the Web pages you read. One way of doing this is to ask yourself the following questions:

- What is the aim of the site? Is it to provide objective information, or to put forward a personal opinion? Is it to advertise individuals or companies? Is the purpose to provide language-learning activities, or just links to other sites which provide these activities? It is important to identify the aims of the site, and then to decide whether it matches up to its aims.

- What authority does the page have? Who wrote the page? Is the name of the author given? (This information is sometimes placed at the bottom of a Web page, together with a contact email address.) Is there any information about the author? (There will sometimes be a link to a personal home page.) What is the name of the company or institution that owns the site where the page is published? Web pages whose addresses end in:

  .ac or *.edu* (as in *http://www.ncl.ac.uk/* or *http://www.cuny.edu*) will be academic institutions;

  .org (as in *http://www.cal.org/* and *http://www.du.org/*) are organizations—often non-profit-making;

  .com or *.co* (as in *http://home.netscape.com/* or *http://www.telegraph.co.uk*) are owned by a company or commercial organization.

Web pages located on Websites such as those run by Geocities are almost certainly the personal home pages of individuals.

Of course, the fact that you have not heard of an author or institution does not mean that the content is not worthwhile, but anonymous pages don't inspire confidence.

- How up to date is the Web page? When was the page first
  written and when was it last updated? (This information is
  usually given at the bottom of a Web page.) If the Web page
  does not appear to have been updated recently, the information
  may be out of date. It is also useful to know how often the
  information is updated to help decide whether it is worth
  visiting the site regularly. This applies particularly to sites that
  deal with news stories and with subjects like shopping or
  computing, where information can quickly become obsolete.

- What is the depth of the page? Some pages have very little
  information. Others lead to many other pages, each of which
  may contain a lot of information or may lead on to further pages
  containing a lot of information. It can be difficult to judge how
  'deep' a site is from just the opening page.

- How accurate is the information in the Web page? Does the page
  have spelling or grammar mistakes? Poor editing of this kind may
  indicate a lack of attention to detail in the content of the page.
  How accurate is the content of the page? If the information is
  important to you, it is worth trying to check at least some of the
  information in the page by reference to other sources.

- How good is the design of the page? To some extent, design
  issues are a matter of taste and fashion. However, a page should
  at least be:
  - easily readable: some combinations of colours are more
    legible than others;
  - easily downloadable: if pages take a long time to **download**
    because they contain large graphics or other media files,
    those files should be essential for the purpose of the page;
  - easily navigable: if there are a lot of pages at a Website, it is
    possible to lose your way as you move around them. Some
    sort of menu or map is important in those cases.

For Websites which give information on evaluating Web pages,
see Appendix E, page 122.

1.5 And the award goes to . . .

LEVEL	**All**
TIME	**60–90 minutes**
AIMS	**To evaluate the appearance and design of Web pages.**
TECHNICAL REQUIREMENTS	One computer per group of 2–3 students, with an Internet connection and a Web browser.

Page	Marks/5	Comments
General appearance Is the page attractive? Why/Why not?		
Clarity Is the page clear? Can you read the information easily?		
Use of colour Are the colours attractive? Do they help to make the information easy to read?		
Ease of use Is it easy to move around the page, or to move on to other pages? Is there anything on the page that distracts your attention from the most important information?		
Presentation and accuracy Are there any spelling or grammar mistakes?		
Multimedia Does the page make good use of pictures, sound, animation, or video? Does the page take a long time to appear?		
Interest Is the page interesting? Why/why not?		
Other criteria		

Photocopiable © Oxford University Press

PREPARATION Identify some well-designed pages—about five or six, depending on how much time you want to spend on this activity—to use in this lesson. See Appendix E ('Activity links', page 121) or our Website at *http://www.oup.com/elt/rbt.internet* for ideas about where to find such pages.

PROCEDURE

1 Tell the students to imagine they are a jury giving awards for the best Websites. Discuss criteria for judging the design and appearance of Web pages, and agree on the different categories that will be given awards.

2 Point out that the students must make notes on their choices and be prepared to justify them. Tell them to make comment sheets like the one below to record their opinions about each of the pages. Use the criteria in the example comment sheet, or substitute others that the students agree on. They should give each page a mark out of five (5 = best) for each of their criteria.

3 The students look at the various Websites you have found for them and make notes.

4 The students then vote, nominating a winning site for each of the categories

5 For each of the categories, a student from a group that voted for the winning page hands over the award, giving reasons why the page won. Another student can accept the award—and even give a short speech if you want to make it more like the Oscars!

VARIATION

The activity can be carried out with Web pages produced by the students or by another class.

1.6 Electric news

LEVEL

Intermediate to advanced

TIME

60 minutes

AIMS

To compare the content of different news Websites, using headlines.

TECHNICAL REQUIREMENTS

One computer per group of 2–3 students, with an Internet connection and a Web browser.

PREPARATION

1 Prepare a list of news Websites. Check these again before the lesson. Suggestions for suitable sites can be found in Appendix E ('Activity links', page 121) or our Website at *http://www.oup.com/elt/rbt.internet*

2 Copy the worksheet below to distribute to students, or download it from our Website and adapt it, or prepare you own.

PROCEDURE

1 Discuss what kind of topics the students expect to find in newspapers (politics, home news, international news, women's pages . . .).

2 Tell students you are going to look at the electronic equivalent of newspapers.

3 Put the students into groups of 2–3 at each computer. Send each group of students to two of the sites you have chosen.

4 Ask students to compare the sites and answer the questions in the worksheet.

Which site has more . . .	News site 1	News site 2
news?		
international news?		
news about the UK (or the US or Australia)?		
sports news?		
news about the arts?		
news about music?		
news about medicine?		
photographs?		
items for women?		
old news (archives)?		
sound-files?		
video?		
What other differences can you see?		

Photocopiable © Oxford University Press

5 Discuss similarities and differences with the students. Ask them which site they would go to first if they wanted to read about:

- *yesterday's football;*
- *a current international event;*
- *something that happened in the US (or UK, or Australia);*
- *something that has been in the news during the previous two weeks;*
- *something that has been in the news during the previous two years;*

or to find

- *a photo to illustrate a topic.*

1.7 Style check

LEVEL	**Upper-intermediate to advanced**
TIME	**60 minutes**
AIMS	**To compare the style and content of articles on the same topic in different news Websites.**
TECHNICAL REQUIREMENTS	One computer per group of 2–3 students, with an Internet connection and a Web browser.

PREPARATION

1 Prepare a list of news Websites. Check these again before the lesson, and choose some news items which are reported in at least two sites. Suggestions for suitable sites can be found in Appendix E ('Activity links', page 121) or our Website at *http://www.oup.com/elt/rbt.internet*

PROCEDURE

1 Ask the students to predict any differences they would expect to find in content and style between different news Websites. Use the worksheet below for ideas if necessary.

2 Tell the students to prepare their own worksheet of relevant points, based on the one provided.

3 Put the students into groups of 2–3 at each computer. Send each group to look at two different reports of one of the news items you have chosen.

4 The students look at the news items on both sites and note down similarities and differences, using their worksheet.

5 Discuss the similarities and differences with the students. Encourage students to think of the cultural, social, or political factors which may have influenced the style and content of the articles.

VARIATION

One advantage of using online news resources is the easy availability of sites from different countries. You could focus on cross-cultural comparisons, comparing, for example, the topics which are of major concern in the students' own country to the main concerns of other countries.

NOTES

The differences will depend on the sites and the topic chosen, but generally, likely differences are:

a the length of the articles (suggesting that one newspaper is giving the news item more prominence, perhaps because the item is of more importance in one country than another—if the newspapers are published in different countries);

b there may be more reported speech in one article than the other (suggesting that the reporter is focusing more on the people involved than on the facts);

	Electronic newspaper 1	Electronic newspaper 2
Are the headlines the same?		
Are there any photos to accompany the article? Are they the same?		
Are the captions to the photos different?		
Are the stories the same length?		
Is the beginning of the story the same in each newspaper?		
Is the conclusion the same?		
Does one story have more direct speech than the other?		
Are the same facts reported in both articles?		
Do the articles emphasize different aspects of the story?		
Is one article more 'personal' than the other? Is one more 'factual'?		
Is one article easier to understand than the other? Is the language easier?		

c one article may have shorter sentences and/or less specialized vocabulary (suggesting that one is written for an audience that knows about the topic, while the other is for a more general audience).

1.8 With a pinch of salt

LEVEL

Upper-intermediate to advanced

TIME

45 minutes

AIMS

To practise critically evaluating information available on the Web.

TECHNICAL REQUIREMENTS

One computer per group of 2–3 students, with an Internet connection and a Web browser.

PREPARATION

1 Choose a controversial topic, which is likely to provoke strong views. 'Smoking' is a good example. Search for and compile a list of sites expressing strong personal views or vested interests. Some suggestions for 'smoking'are included in Appendix E ('Activity links', page 121) and on our Website at *http://www.oup.com/elt/rbt.internet*

2 Copy the worksheet, or prepare your own version.

PROCEDURE

1 Discuss how you might evaluate the information in a document you found on the Web. Ask for suggestions and write them on the board or the OHP.

2 Give the students the worksheet with the evaluation checklist.

3 Discuss what students might look for on the Web pages to answer the questions on the worksheet.

4 Elicit phrases useful for commenting on the questions. Examples might include:

I don't know/can't tell how accurate the information is.
The information seems/appears to be accurate.
The author's name appears/doesn't appear in the document.
His/her qualifications are . . . I can't find his/her qualifications.
The document was written on . . . /updated on . . .
He/she works for . . . I don't know who he/she works for.
I don't know why the document is on the Web. I think the document is on the Web because . . . /so as to . . .
The document seems to me to be quite accurate/inaccurate.

5 Put students into groups of 2–3. Send them to look at the sites you found. Ask them to complete the worksheet.

6 Conduct a feedback session based on the students' comments. Discuss any other questions the students come up with. Agree

with them a set of criteria to be used in evaluating Web pages in future.

	Comments
How accurate is the information? How do you know?	
Who provides the information?	
How much do they know about the topic?	
Is the information objective?	
Is more than one side of the argument presented?	
How up-to-date is the information?	
(Add your own questions)	
What is your opinion of this Web document?	

Photocopiable © Oxford University Press

FOLLOW-UP   Students can choose their own topic, and find their own documents to evaluate. They can publish their evaluations on the institution's network, or print them out and display them.

NOTE   Web pages can also be evaluated for their appearance, and it is important to carry out this kind of evaluation as well if your students are going to produce their own Web pages. For more details, see 1.5, 'And the award goes to . . .', page 34.

Communicating

As well as a source of information, computers are an increasingly important means of communication, using the following Internet resources.

- **Email** is the most common way of communicating on the Internet.

- As well as email to individuals, messages can be sent to groups of people who belong to **discussion lists**. These are often closed lists (i.e. you have to ask to join them) and provide a forum for discussion for particular groups of users or on particular topics. Examples of discussion lists for teachers include TESLCA-L (on computers for language learning) and NETEACH (on the Web for language learning).

- **Newsgroups** are similar to discussion lists because people make contributions to the discussion by email, but the discussions can be read using some Web browsers or by Newsgroup software. They are usually open so that anyone can contribute without having to ask for membership.

- Text-**conferencing** allows text which is typed on one computer to appear almost immediately on another computer, rather like 'simultaneous' email. The most common form of this is **IRC** (**Internet Relay Chat**), which is a simple way of communicating with others via the Internet, either by joining existing discussions, or by setting up your own private discussion group. Other forms include **MOO**s, which are usually closed discussions for particular groups of people or on particular topics. SchMOOze University is an example of a MOO for language teachers and their students. See Appendix D1, page 115, for useful Web addresses.

- **Whiteboarding** allows two or more computers in different places to display the same picture or document, allowing users at any of the computers to make changes which will appear simultaneously on all the computers.

- Audio- and video-**conferencing** allow communication between users on different computers by means of speech and video, rather like telephoning using the Internet.

This section provides practice in using some of these means of communication.

1.9 Lurking detectives

LEVEL Lower-intermediate and above

TIME 30 minutes

AIMS **To introduce students to the etiquette of discussion lists.**

TECHNICAL REQUIREMENTS One computer per group of 2–3 students, with an Internet connection and email. Ideally each student or group of students should have their own email address.

PREPARATION

1 Some time before the lesson, subscribe to one or more email discussion lists, to get an idea of their content. Choose some you feel are suitable for your students. Before this lesson, show students how to subscribe so they have several emails in their mailbox by the time the lesson starts. Details of suitable email lists are shown in Appendix E ('Activity links', page 121) and on our Website at *http://www.oup.com/elt/rbt.internet*

2 Make copies of the worksheets provided.

PROCEDURE

1 Tell the students that they are going to read messages from an email list discussing various topics. Explain that there are certain guidelines which people should follow when sending a message to these discussion lists. Your students are going to check whether people keep to these guidelines.

2 Tell students to complete Part 1 of the worksheet.

3 Tell students to read Part 2 of the worksheet. Then discuss the guidelines about writing to a discussion list.

4 Put the students into groups of 2–3 at the computers, and tell them to open and read the email messages they have received from the list. Ask them to answer the questions in Part 3 of the worksheet. When they have answered all of the questions, or read all of the messages and answered as many of the questions as they can, they should tell you.

5 Discuss the students' findings. Did the contributors to the list keep to the guidelines?

6 Discuss any questions the students have (for example, about **smileys** or abbreviations they found in the messages).

FOLLOW-UP Once students have monitored a list, the next step is to contribute to one.

NOTE Further information about **netiquette** is available on subscription to most discussion lists. A search on the Web for *netiquette* will also turn up lots of information.

Part 1

Do you know what the following mean?	
email	
discussion list	
subject	
signature	
lurk	
flame	
smiley or emoticon	
: -)	
: - (	
; -)	

Photocopiable © Oxford University Press

Part 2

Netiquette

1 Use a correct subject-line for your message. For example:

   Subject: Titanic

2 If you reply to a message using the reply button, your reply should automatically include a subject-line based on the subject-line of the message you are replying to. For example:

   Subject: Re: Titanic.

   If the subject doesn't appear automatically, type it in.

3 Include your signature at the bottom of the message. For example:

   T.Blair@gov.uk, The Management, Downing Street

4 Use capitals only to emphasize a point or to indicate a title or heading.

5 If you reply to a message, don't include all of the original message—just include enough to make it clear what your reply refers to. Show which lines are from the original message, and which from your reply (you usually do this using >). Show where

you have cut out parts of the original message (you usually do this using ... or by writing 'snip'). For example:

>... *Does anyone know where to find the CD?*
I do.

6 Be careful if you try to make a joke—use a smiley if you do. For example:

I can work miracles : -)

7 If you feel angry, don't write a message. **Flaming** (i.e. writing an angry message) is always a mistake. Wait until you no longer feel angry!

Photocopiable © Oxford University Press

Part 3

Can you find a message which . . .	The name of the sender, and the date of the message
includes the subject of the message?	
shows in the subject-line that it is a reply to a previous message?	
does *not* include a subject?	
makes a joke?	
includes a flame?	
uses : -) , : - (, or ; -) ?	
uses a different smiley or emoticon?	
includes some of the original message in the reply?	
includes *all* of the original message in the reply?	

Photocopiable © Oxford University Press

1.10 Electronic holidays

LEVEL	**All**
TIME	**30 minutes**
AIMS	**To practise writing and sending electronic cards.**
TECHNICAL REQUIREMENTS	One computer per group of 2–3 students, with an Internet connection, a Web browser, and email. Each student or group needs an email address.

PREPARATION

1 Find some sites offering suitable electronic greetings cards. Example sites are listed in Appendix E ('Activity links', page 121) and on our Website at *http://www.oup.com/elt/rbt.internet*

2 Check the sites before the lesson. If you have time, send each of the students an electronic postcard before the lesson, so they have an example waiting for them when they open their email.

PROCEDURE

1 Elicit from the students some messages they might write in a card for the relevant holiday or festival. Write some examples on the board.

2 Give each student the email addresses of one or more other students in the class.

3 If you had time to send the students a card before the class, tell them to open their email and show them how to look at the card they have received.

4 Send the students to one of the greetings cards sites you have prepared, and demonstrate how to send a card.

5 Tell students to send a card to their classmates.

6 After the students have done this, discuss any problems they had with either the procedure, the technology, or the language. Ask them to describe the card they chose, and say why they chose it.

7 Either allow the students to open their emails and look at the cards they have been sent, or tell them to look at them later if they have access to computers outside class.

FOLLOW-UP

1 Elicit from the students some messages they might write on birthday cards to their friends. Write some examples on the board. Suggest that they send a card whenever anyone has a birthday in the class.

2 Make a list of the students in the class, their email addresses, and their dates of birth. Put it on the noticeboard. Ask for volunteers to check the birthdays each week and remind the students to send cards to whoever has a birthday the following week.

VARIATION	The cards could be sent to students in other classes or schools. Lists of email addresses and birthdays can be exchanged between classes and schools for this purpose.
NOTE	This activity could be done when there is a holiday or festival when people usually send each other cards.

1.11 Post it

LEVEL	**Elementary and above**
TIME	**30 minutes initially**
AIMS	**To encourage students to use electronic discussion lists; to set up a useful communication channel for the class.**
TECHNICAL REQUIREMENTS	One computer per group of 2–3 students, with an Internet connection, a Web browser, and email. Students should have access to computers outside class time.
PREPARATION	Set up a discussion list before the class. Details of free Internet-based lists are found in Appendix E ('Activity links', page 121) and on our Website at *http://www.oup.com/elt/rbt.internet*

PROCEDURE

1 Give the students details of the discussion list, and explain to them how to join the list.

2 Once they have joined, students must each post a message to the list, asking one question about English grammar, vocabulary, or usage.

3 As homework, ask students to try to answer the questions. They should post their answers to the list.

4 Allow some student discussion before correcting the answers on the list.

5 To keep the discussion going, post occasional homework assignments to the list.

VARIATION 1

1 Suggest that the students set up their own list to discuss issues important to them. Elicit possible subjects.

2 Help the students to set up the lists, and to post an initial message asking for opinions. Encourage the students to subscribe to those of their classmates' lists which interest them.

3 Tell the students that they will be in charge of their discussion lists. Discuss what rules they wish to lay down for the list.

4 We think that getting students to be the editors of discussion lists is good training for understanding the use or control of free speech on the Internet.

VARIATION 2

You might want to use your list for some of the pedagogic functions of the course:

a Students can email questions to it regarding doubts and uncertainties about the material that has been covered, and then you, or designated monitor students, could provide help.

b Preparation work and homework could be mailed to the list.

c If you find students are not using the list as much as you would like, try leaving some tips for a future test on the list and nowhere else!

VARIATION 3

This activity could also be carried out with bulletin boards instead of discussion lists (see Appendix C6, page 114). You could encourage students to think about the differences in communicative style between postings to the bulletin board and postings to the email discussion list.

NOTES

1 If your school has technical staff who run the information technology facilities, consider asking them to set up discussion lists for you.

2 A good source for arguments for many controversial subjects is Trevor Sather and Will Hutton (1999): *Pros and Cons*, London: Routledge.

1.12 That's telling them!

LEVEL

Elementary and above

TIME

30 minutes

AIMS

To give students the chance to participate in a global debate on a contemporary subject.

TECHNICAL REQUIREMENTS

One computer per group of 2–3 students, with an Internet connection, a Web browser, and email.

KNOWLEDGE

Some student knowledge of, and interest in, current affairs.

PREPARATION

Find a news site which has a communications feature, such as a discussion forum. A list of suitable sites can be found in Appendix E ('Activity links', page 121) or on our Website at *http://www.oup.com/elt/rbt.internet*

Check the site before the lesson.

PROCEDURE

1 Ask the students for their opinions about a current news story. Encourage them to compare and contrast their opinions.

2 Tell students they are going to express their views to the world.

3 Put students in groups at the computers. Send them to the site you have prepared, and direct them to the communications facilities.

4 Students then read some of the opinions published on the site. Ask them to find the one that is closest to, and the one that is furthest from, their own opinion.

5 Tell the students to draft an email message to send to the site. Provide assistance as needed while they work on their messages.

6 When they are satisfied with their messages, students should submit them to the site.

VARIATION 1

You could also have students express their opinions live, using chat, if a chat is going on at the time of your class. Note that it is hard to predict how many other people might be in a chat room at any given time, and impossible to control the nature of their messages. Taking students into a live, public-access chat environment is not for the faint of heart!

VARIATION 2

If your students are not interested in current affairs, you could use a site discussing other issues, such as sports, health, or music.

2 Focus on language

Introduction

The focus in this chapter is on vocabulary and grammar practice, but students will continue to develop the core Internet skills introduced in Chapter 1. They will search for examples of vocabulary and grammar, and in some cases store the addresses of pages they have found for future reference. They will have to evaluate the accuracy and reliability of the information they find on some of the pages, and in some Activities they will communicate using email. In addition, however, this chapter emphasizes a number of the other features that make the Internet so appealing for language learning.

How can the Web help the teaching and learning of vocabulary and grammar?

The wealth of language

A wide variety of techniques for using the Web to practise and learn both vocabulary and grammar can fruitfully be applied to the vast amount of language available on the Web. These techniques are often difficult or impossible to use in any other medium. The Web is, for instance, a source of large numbers of examples of vocabulary or grammar. These can provide a simple means of checking the frequency of a word or phrase, or even whether it is used at all, and can provide examples of contexts for a particular item.

Topics

The Web is a rich source of information and material on virtually any topic that your students might be interested in working on. Theme-based work can often be designed around particular Web pages or sites. Students can find pages on topics they would like to explore for project work, and this variety of choice can increase the student's motivation and his or her personal commitment to the task.

Text types

The Web also provides examples of a wide variety of text types, such as descriptions, instructions, narratives, advertisements, and dialogues, and these can be especially useful for practising vocabulary and grammar in a range of contexts.

Culture

The nature of the Web is such that students will frequently encounter information about other cultures, and some of the Activities in this chapter lend themselves easily to work on cross-cultural comparisons.

Resources

The Internet can also be a useful source of more conventional language-teaching resources. Custom-made ESL or EFL materials can be especially useful for practising language at the word or sentence level. Many other kinds of texts can be downloaded and used as the basis for grammar or vocabulary activities in the classroom.

Learning strategies

The work on vocabulary and grammar in this chapter is especially useful for learner training, and for helping students develop appropriate learning strategies. Quizzes done by students as preparation or follow-up for classes can encourage an independent approach to learning. Practice in searching for examples of vocabulary and grammar helps to develop further an independent, active-task approach, and using those examples to check their understanding of vocabulary and grammar provides practice in self-assessment.

Progression

There is some progression in this chapter in terms of the complexity of the Activities, and most users will find that the later Activities in both the Word focus and Grammar focus sections are rather more complex than the earlier ones. In the Grammar focus section, the final tasks that use email and chat look forward to some of the more challenging Activities in Chapter 3.

Word focus

2.1 Word treasures

LEVEL	**Lower-intermediate and above**
TIME	**45–60 minutes**
AIMS	**To encourage students to think about how they record vocabulary.**
TECHNICAL REQUIREMENTS	One computer per group of 2–3 students, with an Internet connection and a Web browser.

PREPARATION

1 Visit some Websites dedicated to vocabulary reference. These might be online dictionaries or thesauruses, or innovative multimedia reference tools. Choose two of the most diverse, which you think will appeal to your students. A selection of suitable sites can be found in Appendix E ('Activity links', page 121) and on our Website at *http://www.oup.com/elt/rbt.internet*

2 Make sure you are familiar with the structure of the sites you choose to use.

PROCEDURE

1 Ask the students to discuss how they record new vocabulary and what information they include in this record.

2 Put the students into small groups to make a list of ten words which they have recently learnt.

3 Send the students to the first of the sites you have chosen, and ask them to find and note down as much information about their ten words as they can. Encourage them to experiment with related words, and to use the full range of features offered.

4 Then ask the students to go to another of your chosen reference sites and follow the same procedure.

5 Discuss with students the kind of information they obtained from each site. Ask them what information they would now record about each word. Could they represent this information graphically, or in a more interesting way?

6 Ask students to think about how they might use some of the techniques employed in the Websites to list new words, in order to build themselves an effective learning resource.

2.2 Tough questions, cross words

LEVEL

All

TIME

15 minutes +

AIMS

To practise vocabulary using online quizzes and crosswords; to assess the usefulness of these resources.

TECHNICAL REQUIREMENTS

One computer per student, or per group of 2–3 students, with an Internet connection and a Web browser.

PREPARATION

1 Visit some sites offering language quizzes, puzzles, and games for students of English, to check their content. Suitable sites can be found in Appendix E ('Activity links', page 121) or on our Website at *http://www.oup.com/elt/rbt.internet*

2 Prepare a list of the quizzes and crosswords most relevant to your students.

PROCEDURE

1 Elicit from the students some vocabulary they have been studying in class recently.

2 Give the students the site addresses you prepared.

3 Ask the students to do some of the quizzes and puzzles. As they do the Activities, they should:

   a note down any interesting or difficult vocabulary;
   b consider what they are learning or being tested on.

4 Tell the students to compare opinions about the quizzes and puzzles they did. *Were they difficult? Interesting? Did they know all of the vocabulary, or did they learn anything new?*

5 Discuss their opinions and deal with any vocabulary problems.

VARIATION

Students can use an existing quiz or crossword as a model to create their own, based on vocabulary that they have recently studied. Some quiz and puzzle sites will accept such submissions and publish them on the site.

NOTES

Teachers will have different opinions about how useful such Activities are and whether they are worth doing in class time. We feel it is useful to draw students' attention to such sites, to allow them to discuss the value of such resources, whether they are used in or out of class time.

2.3 Everywhere you go, always take the weather with you . . .

LEVEL

Intermediate

TIME

30–45 minutes

AIMS

To practise vocabulary related to the theme of the weather.

TECHNICAL REQUIREMENTS

One computer per student or group of 2–3 students, with an Internet connection and a Web browser.

PREPARATION

Find a site or sites which describe the international weather situation. There is a list of examples in Appendix E ('Activity links', page 121) and on our Website at *http://www.oup.com/elt/rbt.internet*

PROCEDURE

1 Elicit vocabulary to describe the weather. Write important expressions on the board.

   Rainy, cloudy, sunny, hot, humid, cold, freezing, predictable, changeable, …

2 Ask the students to imagine they have won a contest and the prize is a trip to an English-speaking country of their choice. Ask the students to choose a country and to guess what the weather is like there at different times of the year. Ask them to consider how that would affect their visit; what clothes they would have to take, what activities they would be able to do, and so on.

3 Then ask students what they think the weather is like now in the country they have chosen.

4 Explain that they are going to look at some Web pages to check the climate in the target country and to check their predictions about the current state of the weather there.

5 In groups, the students go the Websites you have found. They gather information about the climate of their chosen country, and about the current state of the weather.

6 Students discuss their findings, and in particular any results which surprised them.

FOLLOW-UP

Students write a list of items they would take on a visit to the country that week, the kind of activities they would or would not do, and places they would or would not visit because of the weather, with explanations. They could also say which time of year they would prefer to visit the country, and why.

VARIATION

Understanding something of the climate may also be important in interpreting allusions to the weather in some literary texts (for example, 'Now is the winter of our discontent made glorious summer'). Students could search online versions of literary texts (see Appendix E, 'Activity links', page 121) for their references to the weather, and discuss how culture-bound these are.

NOTES

This Activity can be used on its own, but it can also form the first part of a more extended lesson if combined with the next Activity.

2.4 Holiday essentials

LEVEL

Elementary and above

TIME

30 minutes for each part of the activity

AIMS

To practise simple numbers; to practise basic phrases and vocabulary connected with emergencies; to practise language connected with currency conversion; to give an example of thematic vocabulary work.

TECHNICAL REQUIREMENTS

One computer per group of 2–3 students, with an Internet connection and a Web browser.

PREPARATION Find a site or sites which lists international emergency numbers, and another with a currency converter, preferably one that is updated regularly. Suitable sites can be found in Appendix E ('Activity links', page 121) and on our Website at *http://www.oup.com/elt/rbt.internet*

PROCEDURE 1

1 Ask the students: *You need help urgently. Which number do you call?*

2 Then say: *You are in a foreign country and you need urgent help. Which number do you call?*

3 Tell students they are going to find the emergency telephone numbers for various countries.

4 In their groups, the students go to the sites you have chosen, and find the emergency numbers they need.

5 While they are working, go round the groups and ask them to say the phone numbers in English. Correct their pronunciation if necessary.

FOLLOW-UP 1 Practise the vocabulary and phrases students might need if they were making a telephone call to the emergency services. Do a short role play on this subject. For example, choose an English-speaking country and do the following role play, using the correct emergency number:

A *My friend is hurt/My house is on fire/My car has been stolen.*

B *Quick. Phone* **999***.*

A *(Dials and speaks) Hello. I need an ambulance/a fire engine/the police. My address is ….*

PROCEDURE 2

1 Tell the students they are going to check the value of their own currency against the currency of the country they are researching.

2 Send the students to the site you found that has foreign exchange rates.

3 Students should make a note of the date and the current rate of exchange.

4 Ask the students to report their findings to the rest of the class.

5 Tell them to keep a note of the date and the current exchange rate because they are going to return to the site regularly over the next few days/weeks to note any changes.

6 Further checking of the exchange rates can be done for homework if they have access to the Web, or a few minutes can be set aside regularly for this in class.

7 Once they have gathered some information over a period of a few days or weeks, they can be asked to write up a description of the trends they have noticed.

8 Based on their findings, the students could advise when it would be best to buy foreign currency for the country they are researching.

FOLLOW-UP 2   The theme of preparing to travel could be extended to other activities. Students can carry out guided research (using sites provided by you) or independent research (searching for their own resources) to find out different aspects of their chosen country, and prepare different itineraries, or decide what souvenirs and presents would be best to buy.

2.5 Just the job

LEVEL   **Intermediate to advanced**

TIME   **60 minutes**

AIMS   **To practise vocabulary connected with jobs and employment; to compare requirements and conditions for the same job in different countries.**

TECHNICAL REQUIREMENTS   One computer per group of 2–3 students, with Internet connection and Web browser.

PREPARATION   1 Find some sites that provide information about jobs
   a in your country and
   b in a country of interest to your students.

   There are many Websites specializing in recruitment. Check out the more common job titles on the sites you find. A list of initial suggestions for sites is included in Appendix E ('Activity links', page 121) and on our Website at *http://www.oup.com/elt/rbt.internet*

2 Copy the worksheet for each student or group, or prepare your own.

PROCEDURE   1 Elicit from the students as many different job titles as you can. Add any important ones that they miss.

2 Ask them to choose one job title each and to guess, for their own country and for the target country:

   • *what qualifications are needed to get such a job;*
   • *what is involved in doing the job;*
   • *what the pay would be for such a job (remember that pay is likely to vary according to experience);*
   • *where most jobs are likely to be located.*

3 Put students who are going to research the same or similar jobs in groups of 2–3.

4 Send them to the recruitment sites you have found. Tell them to research their chosen job and to complete the worksheet. Students may want to do research on additional

sites, for example, to convert the currencies of the two countries.

5 Discuss the findings, especially the differences between the two countries.

FOLLOW-UP Students could:

- do research on relevant professional organizations, both international and local;
- do comparative research on the cost of living in the two countries;
- find out more about the parts of the country where the jobs are situated.

Job title	
What qualifications do you think are needed for this job?	

What qualifications are actually needed:
    in your country?
    in the other country?	

What did you first imagine would be involved in doing the job?
    in your country?
    in the other country?	

What is actually involved:
    in your country?
    in the other country?	

What does someone doing this job earn (include jobs for people with more and less experience—and give the rate in the local currency and in your own currency):
    in your country?
    in the target country?	

Where are most of the jobs located
    in your country?
    in the target country?	

Photocopiable © Oxford University Press

2.6 I do!

LEVEL	**Intermediate to advanced**
TIME	**45 minutes**
AIMS	**To compare wedding traditions and practices in different countries; to practise the language needed to talk about weddings.**
TECHNICAL REQUIREMENTS	One computer per group of 2–3 students, with Internet connection and Web browser.

PREPARATION

1 Prepare a list of Websites on the topic of weddings in different countries. Check the Websites and identify vocabulary the students might need.

An initial list of sites can be found in Appendix E ('Activity links', page 121) and on our Website at *http://www.oup.com/elt/rbt.internet*

2 Copy the worksheet for each student or group, or prepare your own.

PROCEDURE 1

1 Discuss weddings in your own country. What is a 'traditional' wedding? Are most weddings 'traditional'?

2 Elicit from the students what they know about weddings in other countries.

3 Go through some wedding vocabulary if necessary:

bride/groom, guests, wedding reception, hen night, stag night.

4 Put students in groups and ask them to agree on a country or countries to research. Send them to some of the Websites you found, to gather information about weddings in their chosen country. Ask them to complete the worksheet.

5 The students present their findings to the rest of the class and discuss them. Did they find anything unexpected?

FOLLOW-UP

Students could write up their findings, and possibly publish them on the Web.

VARIATION 1

This kind of activity can usefully be done as an email exchange with students in the other country. Questions, answers and information can be exchanged, or can be placed on a Web page.

VARIATION 2

Students can be asked to talk about their own ideas and wishes about the sort of wedding they would like.

	Your country	*Target country*
Where do people usually get married?		
When do people usually get married?		
What do people do before a wedding?		
What happens at a wedding?		
Can you find a poem for a wedding?		
What sort of music is traditional at a wedding?		

Photocopiable © Oxford University Press

Grammar focus

2.7 Electronic error-checking

LEVEL	Intermediate to advanced
TIME	45 minutes
AIMS	To raise awareness of grammar mistakes made by the students.
TECHNICAL REQUIREMENTS	One computer per group of 2–3 students, with an Internet connection and a Web browser.
PREPARATION	Prepare a list of sentences containing grammar mistakes you have noticed your students making. Add some correct sentences to the list.
PROCEDURE	1 Hand out copies of the list of sentences and give the students a few minutes to decide among themselves which they think are correct.
	2 Ask the students which parts of the sentences they think contain the mistakes. Write one of the sentences on the board, and underline the part illustrating the grammar point you want to revise. Tell students they are going to search for other examples on the Web. They must only search for the underlined part of the sentence. For each sentence on the list, agree with the students which phrase they will search for.

3 Tell the students to carry out the searches and to note the number of 'hits' they get for each grammatical phrase.

4 When they have finished, check the number of hits with the whole class. Discuss whether the number of hits tells you anything about the correctness or otherwise of a particular sentence. Note that a very low number of hits probably indicates incorrect grammar, but it *might* also indicate that the grammatical item is rare.

5 Discuss why there might be examples of incorrect grammar on the Web. (These might be due to typing mistakes by native speakers, or to non-native speakers putting up uncorrected pages on the Web, or to different varieties of English—something might be acceptable in one variety of English but not acceptable in another—or to the language itself being in the process of change: what was previously unacceptable may be becoming acceptable. How much of this kind of discussion you may have will depend on the language level and sophistication of your students.)

FOLLOW-UP Students could keep examples of the grammatical mistakes they make, and put together a list of their own to test their classmates.

Sample list of correct and incorrect grammatical structures

Note that this Activity is most useful if you use examples from your own students' work. The parts of the sentences the students should search for are underlined.

Incorrect sentences	'Hits'	'Genuine' sentences	'Hits'
*He <u>didn't went</u> to the cinema last week.		He <u>didn't go</u> to the cinema last week.	
*<u>Always you do</u> that.		<u>You always do</u> that.	
*He is a <u>too good swimmer</u>.		He <u>is a very good swimmer</u>.	
*He <u>has been here since three years</u>.		He <u>has been here for three years</u>.	
*He <u>ran fastly</u>.		He <u>ran fast</u>.	
*He <u>ran quick</u>.		He <u>ran quickly</u>.	
*He <u>saw not</u> the film.		He <u>didn't see</u> the film.	

2.8 Jembled tuxt

LEVEL	**Intermediate to advanced**
TIME	**45 minutes**
AIMS	**To practise recognizing discourse markers.**

TECHNICAL REQUIREMENTS

One computer per group of 2–3 students, with an Internet connection, a Web browser, and (ideally) a word-processor.

KNOWLEDGE

You will need to know how to save pages from the Web. For some versions of the activity, you will need to know how to save graphics as well as text. See Appendix B2, 'Working offline', page 106, for help with this.

PREPARATION

Save a page from the Web. Load it into a word-processor and jumble up the paragraphs. Print, or distribute electronically, a jumbled copy and the original copy, for each student or group.

PROCEDURE 1

1 Ask students what they would expect to find in the opening and concluding paragraphs of a text on the topic of the page you have saved. Discuss other ways of identifying the order of paragraphs in a text.

2 Put students into groups of 2–3. Give them the jumbled paragraphs. Tell them to work together to identify the correct order of the paragraphs. If students are working electronically, they should open the word-processor document and edit the text there. Stress that students must be ready to explain the reasons for the order they choose.

3 Discuss their answers.

4 Give students the original document or send them to the original page on the Web. Tell them to compare their answer with the original.

5 Answer any questions the students may have after the comparison.

VARIATION 1

The activity can be done with jumbled words in sentences, or jumbled sentences in paragraphs.

VARIATION 2

Graphics may provide important extra information in a text. If this is the case with any of the Web pages, one of the activities can be to match graphics with information in the text.

VARIATION 3

Because of the way in which hyperlinks can be placed in a text, the Web has certain discourse characteristics of its own. To focus on these characteristics:

a Ask students to guess from underlined links what the linked texts will contain.

b Students can then be presented with the pages of linked text and asked to match them to the links.

c Alternatively, ask the students to look at the text on the first page of a Website, or at the beginning of a section in the Website. Ask them then to read a page of text which is linked to that first page. They should then return to the first page and scan it to identify words, phrases, or sentences which could form a suitable link to the linked text.

2.9 Email to myself

LEVEL	**Elementary**
TIME	**20–30 minutes, in each of two lessons**
AIMS	**To practise basic verb tenses.**
TECHNICAL REQUIREMENTS	One computer per group of 2–3 students, with an Internet connection, a Web browser, and email. Students should each have an email address.
PREPARATION	Copy the list of questions provided here, or prepare your own, focusing on language the class has been studying.
PROCEDURE	**Lesson 1**

1 Get the students to answer the following questions:

Please answer the following questions
a What are you doing now?
b How are you feeling?
c What time is it?
d What time did you get up today?
e What are you going to do tonight? . . . etc.

Photocopiable © Oxford University Press

2 When they have finished, check their answers.

3 If necessary, show the students how to send and receive email

messages. Ask them to start a new email message, and address it to themselves.

4 The students write their answers to the questions above as the body of the message.

5 The students send the message to themselves.

LESSON 2

6 The students open the emails they wrote in the previous lesson. They edit the message, along the following lines:

> On Tuesday I was writing an email and I am also doing that today.
>
> On Tuesday I was feeling tired, but today I am feeling happy.
>
> etc.

7 The students send this email to you.

8 Correct and return the emails.

VARIATION

The same Activity could be adapted to practise reported speech by beginning '*On Tuesday I wrote that…*'

2.10 Consequences

LEVEL

Intermediate

TIME

45 minutes

AIMS

To practise reported speech.

TECHNICAL REQUIREMENTS

One computer per group of 2–3 students, with an Internet connection, a Web browser, and Internet Relay Chat.

KNOWLEDGE

You will need to know how to set up an Internet chat room. See Appendix C3, 'Text conferencing', page 113, for help with this.

PREPARATION

1 Set up a chat room for the class before the lesson. Suggestions for possible resources are found in Appendix E ('Activity links', page 121) and on our Website at *http://www.oup.com/elt/rbt.internet*

2 Prepare a set of the consequences 'templates' to give out to students.

PROCEDURE

1 Divide the class into at least six groups, one group for each line in the consequences story. If your class is large, some of the lines can have more than one group. In this case, students can vote on which lines are the best.

2 Give each group one of the consequences 'template' sentences listed below. Explain that they must follow the instructions in

italics to complete the phrases. Draw their attention to the examples.

- *write the name of a famous man* met
  Example: Batman met

- *write the name of a famous woman* in
  Example: Madonna in

- *write the name of a place*
  Example: Ireland

- He asked her *complete the sentence*
  Example: He asked her if she wanted a sweet.

- She replied that *complete the sentence*
  Example: She replied that she was on a diet.

- And the consequence was *complete the sentence*
  Example: And the consequence was he ate all the sweets himself.

3 Have a trial run of the activity with the example sentences:

  a Send the students to the chat room you have created.
  b Ask each group to type a test message.
  c When all the students have arrived in the chat room, ask them to type the example phrase into the chat box. They must NOT press Enter until you say so.
  d When they have all finished typing, tell the students to press Enter.
  e The phrases will appear in random order on the screen. Ask students to read the whole story aloud, in order.

4 Now ask students to write their own phrases into the chat box, following the instructions on the template. Remind them not to press Enter until you tell them. Check every group is doing the task correctly. Correct any language mistakes.

5 Continue as in the trial run.

6 Get students to change templates, and repeat. Continue until all the groups have written at least one of the sentences using reported speech.

VARIATION

Vocabulary or grammar revision games can also be played using this method. You call out a clue, and students enter their suggestions . The first group whose answer appears can then set the next clue.

2.11 Last question please

LEVEL	**Elementary and above**
TIME	**30–45 minutes**
AIMS	**To revise question formation**
TECHNICAL REQUIREMENTS	One computer per group of 2–3 students, with an Internet connection, a Web browser, and Internet Relay Chat.
KNOWLEDGE	You will need to know how to set up an Internet chat room. See Appendix C3, 'Text conferencing', page 113, for help with this.
PREPARATION	Set up a chat room for the class before the lesson. Suggestions for possible resources are found in Appendix E ('Activity links', page 121) and on our Website at *http://www.oup.com/elt/rbt.internet*
PROCEDURE	1 Elicit some questions from the students and check question forms.
	2 Put the students into groups at the computer. Send them to the chat room you have created.
	3 Ask each group to type a test message.
	4 Check that it is clear from the name they are using which students are producing which comment. If necessary, give each group a number, and ask them to preface any comment with that number, or get the students to note down who is in each group.
	5 Ask the class for the name of a famous, living person.
	6 Tell them they are going to interview that person, but they have only been given five minutes. They will only be able to ask ten questions. The groups have to think of good questions to ask the person.
	7 Students type suggested questions into the chat. If the questions are grammatically wrong, disallow them (either by sending a message or by calling out), but do not correct the mistake yet.
	8 Continue until ten correct questions have been submitted.
	9 Discuss with the class the errors in the disallowed questions.
	10 Now inform the class that they have been given another five minutes, and must submit another ten questions. This time, the student groups must decide which questions to accept.
	11 Discuss the resulting questions.
VARIATION	It is possible to 'log' the discussion by saving a copy of it. This could be used to make a copy of the correct and disallowed question forms, which could be used in a revision or consolidation exercise in the following lesson.

3 Focus on language skills

Introduction

The Activities in this chapter provide further practice in the core Internet skills, but focus on the individual language skills of writing, reading, listening, speaking, and translating, as well as providing integrated skills practice.

How can the Web help the teaching and learning of language skills?

Language skills

The Web is a rich source of information in English, and of Web pages that can provide texts for reading practice. There are also increasing numbers of Websites containing material that can be used for listening practice. Such text and audio material can also be used as a stimulus for writing and speaking practice and, naturally, for activities practising integrated skills. This chapter demonstrates how materials available on the Web can be used to provide practice in all of these areas.

Web skills

In addition, the Web itself is organized in such a way that it requires additional reading and writing skills that are rather different from those required for reading conventional, linear text. This chapter therefore provides some practice in the particular reading skills required by hyptertext.

Communication

As in the previous chapters, the Activities use resources based on a wide variety of topics and different types of text, providing practice in important learning strategies. In addition, there is more emphasis in the chapter on practising communication strategies, using a variety of media, and on raising awareness of purpose and audience in communication. The Web is often described as an example of a communications and information technology. Email and text-, audio-, and video-conferencing programs allow the Web to be used for rapid or immediate communication between learners in different classes, schools, towns, and countries. This chapter contains examples of ways in which such programs can be used to provide practice in reading and in communicating through both writing and speaking.

Translation

Translation can be a very effective learning tool, especially in increasing students' awareness of style and of the range of meanings a particular word or phrase can convey. It is also a linguistic skill in its own right and the Web provides ample resources for practising this skill. The Web provides ample resources for practising translation. First, it provides access to a wide range of texts in many languages. Second, many Web pages exist in parallel versions in more than one language, providing opportunities for comparing an original text with its translation. And finally, there are a number of automatic translation tools that can provide useful material for checking and evaluating translations.

Due to the rapid increase in the amount of information on the Web, there is a growing need for translation, and especially for information such as news items to be translated quickly into a variety of languages. The Web therefore not only provides material that can be used for translation practice but also provides a motivation for carrying out translation activities. This chapter makes use of news broadcasts, automatic translations, and home pages in the students' first language to provide practice in translating and interpreting.

Writing focus

3.1 Home on the Net

LEVEL	**All**
TIME	**90–120 minutes (or several lessons)**
AIMS	**To create home pages.**
TECHNICAL REQUIREMENTS	One computer per group of 2–3 students, with an Internet connection, a Web browser, and Web-authoring or word-processing software. You will need a scanner to digitalize photographs, if they are not already digital.
KNOWLEDGE	You will need to know how to create and publish a Web page. See Appendix B4, 'Writing Web pages', page 108, for help with this.
PREPARATION	1 It is a good idea to do Activity 1.5, 'And the award goes to...', page 34, before students create their own Web pages.

2 Find out if any students already have experience of Web page construction. If they have, ask them to monitor and help the less experienced students.

PROCEDURE

1 Tell the students they are going to construct their own personal home page.

2 Brainstorm ideas for content to include on the page. Home pages often contain:

- personal details;
- photographs;
- details about friends, family, and pets;
- information about hobbies;
- a list of links to favourite Websites.

3 Students plan the content of their pages.

4 In small groups, students present their plans to one another, and exchange feedback.

5 Working in groups if necessary, students construct their home pages.

6 When the pages are ready, ask the groups of students to move from computer to computer. They should look at their classmates' sites and comment on what they like and what could be improved.

7 Students return to their own sites and finalize their pages.

8 Check the pages for content and accuracy before publishing them, either on the institution's network or on the Web.

VARIATION 1

A home page for the whole class could also be constructed, linking to the individual home pages.

VARIATION 2

Students could create a Web page on a specific topic. They could plan and carry out a topic-based research and creation project, using the Internet as resource. Before publishing such projects on the Web, be aware that images, sounds and text taken from other Web pages are subject to copyright law, and should not be used without the consent of the originator.

NOTES

There is a danger, especially with younger students, that Web page projects can become too ambitious. Make sure the students break ambitious projects into manageable chunks.

3.2 Valentine's Day

LEVEL	**Intermediate and above**
TIME	**45–60 minutes**
AIMS	**To use the Internet to produce Valentine's Day cards.**
TECHNICAL REQUIREMENTS	One computer per group of 2–3 students, with an Internet connection, a Web browser, and a word-processing program.
KNOWLEDGE	Students will need to know how to use a Web directory or search engine. They will also need at least basic word-processing skills.
PREPARATION	Find some examples of love poems on the Web. Use a Web directory or search engine to do this. Some suggestions are included in Appendix E ('Activity links', page 121) and on our Website at *http://www.oup.com/elt/rbt.internet*

PROCEDURE

1 Ask the students if they ever read poetry. If they do, ask them for their favourite poem (in any language). Ask them if they know any love poetry. Introduce the topic of Valentine's Day. Tell the students they are going to design a Valentine's Day card.

2 Put the students into groups of 2 or 3 and send them to look at some of the love poems you have found. Alternatively, if their searching skills are good, set them the task of finding love poems themselves.

3 Students should select a few verses from the poems they read, and cut and paste the verses into a word-processor file.

4 Regroup the students so they are working with different people. Make sure each group has access to all the verses selected in the previous stage.

5 Students must work in their new groups to design a Valentine's Day card using the verses. They must decide between them which of all the verses are most suitable for the purpose.

6 Students then design the card in a word-processing program, using the poetry and adding their own touches.

7 If they like, the students can mail the cards, in either printed or electronic form.

VARIATIONS

Similar seasonal work could be carried out using classic literature. For example, references to Christmas, New Year, Hannukah, etc. could be compared and commented on. Online text archives provide searchable versions of non-copyrighted texts: see Appendix E ('Activity links', page 121) and our Website at *http://www.oup.com/elt/rbt.internet* for suggestions.

NOTES

1 If the cards are to be delivered electronically, and students want to retain their anonymity, it is useful to have an extra 'fictitious'

email address, for example, *astudent@email.com*. Set this up beforehand and then get the students to use it in turn to send their Valentines.

2 If the class has a class discussion list or bulletin board (see 1.11, 'Post it', page 47), students can use it to speculate on who sent what!

3.3 The play's the thing

LEVEL	**Intermediate to upper-intermediate**
TIME	**60 minutes**
AIMS	**To practise writing dialogue using Internet Relay Chat.**
TECHNICAL REQUIREMENTS	One computer per group of 2–3 students, with an Internet connection, a Web browser, Internet Relay Chat, and word-processor.
KNOWLEDGE	You will need to be able to set up an Internet chat group or room. Suggestions for possible resources are included in Appendix E ('Activity links', page 121) and on our Website at *http://www.oup.com/elt/rbt.internet*

You will also need to check that you can record the chat session, either by keeping a log, if the chat program supports this, or by cutting and pasting the chat text into a word-processing program. If you have a large class, you can set up more than one chat room. |
| **PREPARATION** | Set up an Internet chat group or room. Prepare the beginning of two short, dramatic example dialogues. |
| **PROCEDURE** | 1 Write a couple of lines of sample dialogue on the board. Elicit possible continuations.

2 Explain to the students that they are going to write a dialogue, using the chat program. Discuss the scene and characters.

3 Divide the students into groups of 2–3. Assign each group one character. If you have a large class, assign the groups to different chat 'rooms'.

4 Tell the students to log into the chat. If possible, they should log in with the name of their character. Ask all groups to type a test message.

5 Put the beginning of the dialogue on the board. Invite students to continue the dialogue in the chat room.

6 Students develop the dialogue. Make sure that you, or a designated group of students, are keeping a record of the dialogue as it progresses.

7 When the dialogue is finished, make sure that all groups have a |

copy of the saved text. They open this text in a word-processing program, and make any final changes.

FOLLOW-UP 1 Students act out the dialogue.

FOLLOW-UP 2 For homework, students could write the next scene, following a prompt such as *Later that day . . . .*

VARIATION 1 Students could write the dialogue of an imaginary encounter between historical personalities.

VARIATION 2 Students who are reading a novel could choose an event from the book and write the imaginary interior dialogue of the characters.

VARIATION 3 Students could take an existing literary work or film, and write alternative versions of certain scenes.

NOTES Internet Relay Chat programs are fairly easy to use, but with a large number of groups writing suggestions at the same time, it is better to have someone, either yourself or a student, act as a moderator.

Sample scene and dialogue:

Breakfast. Mother and father and two children. One of the children got home very late the previous evening. Write the conversation at breakfast. Begin with:

Dad: So, what time did you get in last night?

3.4 Alternative school guide

LEVEL Advanced

TIME 60–90 minutes

AIMS **To write an informal guide to an educational establishment.**

TECHNICAL REQUIREMENTS One computer per student, or per group of 2–3 students, with an Internet connection, a Web browser, and Web-authoring or word-processing software.

PREPARATION 1 Prepare a list of sites giving unofficial, informal descriptions of educational establishments. For institutions in the UK, see Appendix E ('Activity links', page 121) and our Website at *http://www.oup.com/elt/rbt.internet* for suitable sites. Before the lesson, visit the site and choose one educational institution for the students to look at.

2 Copy the question grid provided, or design your own.

PROCEDURE

1 Tell the students they are going to read an unofficial description of an educational establishment. Send students to the site you have chosen.

2 The students read the text and answer the questions in the grid.

3 When the students have finished, discuss their answers to the questions.

4 Ask the students to follow the style of the university description and write a similar text for their own educational institution.

5 Students compare their versions, and agree on one, definitive final version.

6 Discuss with students how their work would compare with a more official description of their institution.

NOTES

If possible, the students could publish their description on the Web pages of their educational institution.

Look at the description of the institution and answer the following questions:	
What are the main positive features of the institution?	
What other features strike you?	
What sections is the description divided into?	
How are the sections introduced?	
What features of the sentences do you notice?	
Choose five words or phrases which typify the style of the passage.	
Who is the text mainly written for?	
Overall, how would you describe the style of the text?	

Photocopiable © Oxford University Press

3.5 'The Truth is out there'

LEVEL Intermediate and above

TIME 90–120 minutes

AIMS To practise narrative writing.

TECHNICAL REQUIREMENTS One computer per group of 2–3 students, with an Internet connection, a Web browser, and a word-processing program.

PREPARATION Find the Website of a television programme which is popular with your students. Check that the site has episode guides. The site used here as an example is that of *The X-Files*: you can find the address in Appendix E ('Activity links', page 121) or on our Website at *http://www.oup.com/elt/rbt.internet*

PROCEDURE
1 Elicit which students watch *The X-Files*. Get students to describe a typical episode and the style of the series.
2 Put the students into groups of 2–3 at each computer. Explain that they are going to read the plot of an episode.
3 Send the students to the site. The students choose an episode and read the episode guide.
4 Tell the students they are going to have the opportunity to create their own *X-Files* plot. Ask them to decide, in their groups, on what will happen in their episode. They should then write an episode guide, using the ones on the site as a model. Help them with vocabulary and style.
5 Once students have finished and saved their texts, make sure they are accessible to all the groups by, for example, putting them on a **public drive**.
6 Students read the episodes written by other groups and decide which episodes they would most like to watch.

FOLLOW-UP 1 If a series of the programme is currently showing on television, students could be asked to watch the next episode and summarize it in a further episode guide. They could then compare this with the guide published on the Website.

FOLLOW-UP 2 If students enjoy this type of activity, draw their attention to the fan-fiction resources available on the Web, where fans write imaginary episodes of their favourite television programmes. A search for the phrase "fan fiction" together with the name of a programme will often prove fruitful.

VARIATION If access to the Internet is not possible for several machines at the same time, the pages with the episode guides can be printed out.

NOTES

1 The idea could be adapted for another television programme, and a Net search carried out to find sites with information about the programme.

2 This activity presumes that the chosen programme will be shown on a television channel that students have access to. If not, episodes may be available for purchase on video and could be used to introduce the programme to students.

3.6 What the critics say

LEVEL

Pre-intermediate and above

TIME

45–60 minutes

AIMS

To write a book review and publish it on the Internet.

TECHNICAL REQUIREMENTS

One computer per student or group of 2–3 students, with an Internet connection, a Web browser, and a word-processor.

PREPARATION

Find a Website which publishes, and ideally accepts, reader submissions of book reviews. Ideas for sites to look at can be found in Appendix E ('Activity links', page 121) or on our Website at *http://www.oup.com/elt/rbt.internet*

PROCEDURE

1 Ask the students if they have ever read a book review online.

2 Direct the students to your chosen site, and ask them to find some books which interest them. They can browse by category, search for a particular author, or follow the suggestions of the site editors.

3 Ask students to find a review on the site of one of the books they have chosen. Discuss the style of the reviews with them. Were they written by professional reviewers or by members of the public?

4 Ask students what books they have read recently. Tell them to see if any of these books are to be found on the site.

5 Ask students to write a review of a book they have read which is listed on the site. Students can peer-check each other's writing and make editing suggestions.

6 Students edit their texts and, if the site permits, submit them to the book site to be published.

VARIATION 1

If the students are using a language coursebook, they could write a review of it for prospective teachers and students.

VARIATION 2

Students can use the search engine of the book site to find out which authors and books in their own language have been published in translation in English. They could then write their review of one of these books. In this way, they are helping to publicize an aspect of their own culture.

VARIATION 3

If your school has its own Website, reviews of books could be published on it.

Reading focus

3.7 Virtual kitchen

LEVEL

Intermediate

TIME

15–30 minutes

AIMS

To find specific information on a Website; to practise vocabulary associated with food and nutrition.

TECHNICAL REQUIREMENTS

One computer per student or group of 2–3 students, with an Internet connection and a Web browser.

PREPARATION

1 Choose one of the many Websites dedicated to health and nutrition. Examples are listed in Appendix E ('Activity links', page 121) and on our Website at *http://www.oup.com/elt/rbt.internet*

2 Using the information on the site, prepare a quiz, like the example given overleaf.

PROCEDURE

1 Ask the students for the names of various kinds of food and write them on the board. Ask them what they know about health issues related to food, such as nutritional values and storage requirements.

2 Give students the quiz you have prepared. Ask them if they can answer any of the questions. They should write in any answers they think they know. Tell students that the answers to all of the questions are available online.

3 Send students to the site you have chosen, and ask them to complete the quiz, making sure they check any of the answers they have already written.

4 While they do this, students should note any vocabulary that is new or difficult for them.

5 When all the students have finished, discuss their results. Deal with any vocabulary problems they encountered, and discuss any unusual facts they learnt.

6 Tell students to prepare a short quiz of their own, using unusual facts from the Website.

7 Students can use their quizzes to test the rest of the class.

Food quiz

Look at the questions below. How many answers can you find on the Web?

Should you store yoghurt on the shelves or in the doors of your fridge?	
Can you freeze yoghurt?	
Apples soften faster outside the fridge than inside. By how much? Twice as fast? Five times as fast?	
If you eat vegetables and cheese together, it is very good for your teeth. But what kind of cheese do you need?	
Are brown eggs better for you than white eggs?	
How long will carrots last in a fridge?	
How long can you keep a cooked turkey in a fridge?	
Can you freeze ham?	
We need 50 nutrients for good health. How many of these can be found in milk?	
Do eggs contain vitamin A?	

Photocopiable © Oxford University Press

VARIATION 1   Instead of being sent to a particular site, students could find the information by performing Web searches. In this case, they should note the source of the information they find. If two groups find conflicting information, they should think about why conflicting information might exist on the Web, and, if necessary, argue as to which is more accurate!

VARIATION 2   This activity could be adapted for many different subjects, such as sports, history, politics, or entertainment.

3.8 Step by step

LEVEL	**Lower-intermediate to intermediate**
TIME	**30–60 minutes**
AIMS	**To practise reading and carrying out instructions for making things.**

TECHNICAL REQUIREMENTS
One computer per group of 2–3 students, with an Internet connection, a Web browser, and, optionally, a printer.

PREPARATION

1 Find some sites which give instructions for making things. Some suggestions are included in Appendix E ('Activity links', page 121) and on our Website at *http://www.oup.com/elt/rbt.internet*

2 Choose sets of instructions which you think will appeal to your students.

3 If you decide to have the students carry out the instruction in class, you will need to prepare all of the materials and equipment required.

PROCEDURE

1 Revise with the students the language of instructions. Ask students what type of instructions they follow in their daily lives.

2 Elicit the meaning of some of the vocabulary items you think they might have problems with in the instructions you have chosen.

3 Send students, in groups, to the sites you have chosen. Students should read through the instructions, trying to visualize each step. They should make a note of any language problems they encounter.

4 The groups compare any language problems they had.

5 Bring the whole class together to deal with any remaining language problems.

6 Depending on the facilities available in the classroom, you might want the students to complete the activity by carrying out the instructions in class—or you may prefer to have them do this at home. Either way, after they have followed the instructions, they should give a short presentation to the class, evaluating the instructions they were given. How easy were they to follow? Did they provide all the necessary information?

3.9 Academia

LEVEL	**Advanced**
TIME	**60 minutes**
AIMS	**To practise the language of school subjects; to compare some aspects of different educational systems.**

TECHNICAL REQUIREMENTS

One computer per group of 2–3 students, with an Internet connection and a Web browser.

The activity is written for students interested in going to university. The variation provides a version for students who might have an interest in other types of educational institution.

PREPARATION

1 Prepare a selection of Websites giving information about educational institutions and their locations, and educational placement services or agencies. Ideas for such sites can be found in Appendix E ('Activity links', page 121) and on our Website at *http://www.oup.com/elt/rbt.internet*

2 Copy the worksheet provided, or design your own.

PROCEDURE

1 Ask the students what subject or subjects they would like to study at university.

2 Discuss where they want to study, and whether they will have any problems in being admitted to study their chosen subject at their chosen institution.

3 Ask them if they know how the university applications procedure works in the UK. Check that they understand what GCSEs and A-Levels are. Ask them to guess how the grades of these qualifications relate to the grades that are awarded in their own system.

4 Ask them to think of two or three places in Britain where they might want to live and study their chosen subjects. Explain that they are going to check:

a whether the subject they want to study is offered in the places they are interested in;

b the entrance requirements for their chosen subject and location;

c how many other locations offer the same subject;

d whether they can find any places they hadn't thought of originally where they might like to study;

e whether they can find any other useful information about the universities or towns they are interested in.

5 Give students the list of Websites you have chosen, and the worksheet. Students should choose which of the links to visit, and use the information they find to complete the worksheet.

6 Discuss what the students found out about the education system, or about particular towns/cities or universities, or subjects or information that surprised them.

FOLLOW-UP   Students could write an account of the important points they discovered.

Subject	University 1	University 2	University 3
What are the entrance requirements for the subject you have chosen? Are they high, low, or average?			
Do the guides make positive or negative comments about the location, the university, or the subject department?			
Does the university Website provide useful information about the town/city, the university, or the department?			
Does the university year seem to be the same as the university year in your country? Does the academic year start at the same time as yours?			
Can you find out anything useful or interesting about the town/city or region?			

Photocopiable © Oxford University Press

3.10 Play it again, Sam

LEVEL   **Elementary and above**

TIME   **60 minutes**

AIMS   **To practise reading for specific information.**

TECHNICAL   One computer per student or group of 2–3 students, with Internet
REQUIREMENTS   connection and newsgroup software.

PREPARATION   1 Familiarize yourself with newsgroups before starting this
                          activity: subscribe to several and choose some which are likely
                          to be of interest to your students. This activity uses a music

newsgroup as its example. Details of this and other newsgroups can be found in Appendix E ('Activity links', page 121) and on our Website at *http://www.oup.com/elt/rbt.internet*

PROCEDURE

1 Ask the students, in pairs, to write down three hobbies or interests they have.

2 Get the students to share this information.

3 Tell the students you are going to give an example of a newsgroup which exchanges information about music.

4 Tell the students to go to the newsgroup you have chosen, and look at some of the postings.

5 Send students to the list of available newsgroups, and ask them to find one which relates to an interest of theirs, and subscribe to it.

6 Ask students to read the postings and try to find some information about their interest which they did not know before.

7 Students report back to the class on the newsgroups they have looked at, giving their assessment of the quality and type of information available.

FOLLOW-UP

Once students have become familiar with a particular newsgroup, they can then compose a message, and become active newsgroup members.

NOTES

There are thousands of newsgroups, some very active and some not. The actual list of groups can seem a bit daunting at first, but it is worth persevering, since there seems to be a newsgroup for just about every imaginable hobby or interest.

Listening focus

3.11 Breaking news

LEVEL

Intermediate and above

TIME

30–45 minutes

AIMS

To practise listening for detail in news broadcasts.

TECHNICAL REQUIREMENTS

One computer per student or group of 2–3 students, with an Internet connection, a Web browser, a sound card, speakers, and, optionally, headphones and a headphone splitter (to allow two or more headphones to be connected to the same computer). For most sites you will need special browser plugin software to listen to the audio.

PREPARATION

Choose two news sites which have audio files of news broadcasts. Suggestions for possible sites are in Appendix E ('Activity links', page 121) and on our Website at *http://www.oup.com/elt/rbt.internet*

Just before the lesson, go to the sites and listen to the current audio news to check it is suitable for the task.

PROCEDURE

1 Tell the students they are going to listen to two different radio news broadcasts. They should listen carefully, and make notes of the differences between the two programmes.

2 Send students to the news sites you have chosen. The students listen to the news broadcasts and make notes on the differences. They also make notes of any language that they would like clarified.

3 Discuss the results with the students. Which student, or group of students, heard the most differences?

4 Discuss with students the advantages and disadvantages of listening to radio programmes on the Internet. Possible advantages include:

- students can choose to repeat the whole or a small part of the programme as many times as they wish;
- it is possible to listen to up-to-date radio programmes without having to hear them at a scheduled time;
- it is possible to 'tune in' to radio stations from around the world.

Possible disadvantages include the size of the phone bill students might run up if they are using a dial-up connection!

3.12 Audiobooks

LEVEL

Upper-intermediate to advanced

TIME

30–45 minutes

AIMS

To introduce students to a new aspect of literature studies; to practise listening comprehension.

TECHNICAL REQUIREMENTS

One computer per student, or per group of 2–3 students, with an Internet connection, a Web browser, a sound card, speakers and, optionally, headphones and a headphone splitter.

PREPARATION

Find a site with suitable extracts from audiobooks, or audio files of literary texts. Ideas for sites which offer these can be found in Appendix E ('Activity links', page 121) and on our Website at *http://www.oup.com/elt/rbt.internet*

PROCEDURE

1 Discuss with the students what they like to read. Write on the board a list of the kinds of text they mention (for example, short stories, adventure stories, horror stories, biographies, novels, poems).

2 Ask if students enjoy being read to. Introduce the concept of the 'audiobook'.

3 Tell them they are going to go to a site that has extracts from audio versions of short stories, books, and poems. Before they go to the site, they should decide what sort of material they would like to listen to.

4 The students then go to the site, and choose an extract to listen to.

5 They note the name of the extract and of the author. They listen to part of it (maybe two minutes, as some of the extracts can be quite long), and make a note of the main points.

6 When they have finished, they write down the title and author, and a brief 'synopsis' of what they have listened to. They decide whether they would like to listen to the whole 'audiobook', whether they would like to read the whole of the work, and whether they would recommend it to the rest of the class. Ask students to give the extracts marks out of ten.

7 The resulting reports should be made available to all the students, in either electronic or printed form.

8 Discuss with the students what they liked and what they found difficult about the activity.

9 To see what was most popular with the students, write a table on the board showing the types of text they listened to, the titles, the authors, and the scores they gave them.

3.13 Listen and link

LEVEL

Intermediate to advanced

TIME

60 minutes

AIMS

To improve listening skills; to create hypertexts of related materials.

TECHNICAL REQUIREMENTS

One computer per group of 2–3 students, with an Internet connection, a Web browser, a sound card, speakers, and, optionally, headphones and a headphone splitter (to allow two or more headphones to be connected to the same computer).

KNOWLEDGE

Students should be competent at searching for information, and able to author Web pages.

PREPARATION	Choose a news Website with audio broadcasts. Check out key sites for supplementary materials relevant to current news stories, such as maps and biographies.

PROCEDURE	

1 Ask students what advantages news on the Web has over television or radio news. If students do not suggest it, introduce the idea of the value of links to relevant information.

2 Ask students to predict what items are likely to be in the current news.

3 Explain that they are going to listen to a news broadcast on the Web. They do not have to understand every detail of the broadcast, but they will need to be able to create *three* links to background material.

4 Send the students to the site you have chosen.

5 They listen to the news and make a note of the main items mentioned.

6 In groups, they decide which items a listener might want to have more information about. They search for this information, and make a note of three key URLs.

7 In their groups, they create a Web page, and insert a link to the news audio clip. Under the link to the clip, they put in links to the relevant sites they have found.

8 Each group then looks at the links the others have selected. Discuss the results. Do students think it is possible to predict what additional information a listener to the news might require? How is the Internet transforming attitudes to news?

3.14 Listen and look

LEVEL	Intermediate to advanced
TIME	60 minutes
AIMS	**To introduce the students to the Web as a resource for audio and visual materials; to encourage students to work creatively with audio and visual materials.**
TECHNICAL REQUIREMENTS	One computer per group of 2–3 students, with an Internet connection, a Web browser, a sound card, speakers, and, optionally, headphones and a headphone splitter.
KNOWLEDGE	Students should be competent at performing Internet searches.
PREPARATION	1 Put together some interesting images. These can be photos, posters, OHTs, or Web pages. Select some pieces of contrasting music to accompany the images.

2 Find some sites rich in interesting images, and some which have lots of sound files. See Appendix E ('Activity links', page 121) and on our Website at *http://www.oup.com/elt/rbt.internet* for suggestions.

PROCEDURE

1 Show the images you have prepared, while at the same time playing the contrasting pieces of music. Ask students to discuss which piece of music goes best with each illustration, and why.

2 Send students to the resource sites you have prepared, or ask them to find their own. They should try to find sound files and image files which complement each other.

3 Each group gives a short presentation of the music–image combinations they have chosen, explaining their choices.

4 More technically advanced classes could save the audio links and associated pictures onto a Web page. Note that copyright restrictions may be violated if you make such pages publicly available on the Internet.

Speaking focus

3.15 Fingers crossed

LEVEL

Upper-intermediate to advanced

TIME

30 minutes

AIMS

To talk about superstitions in different cultures.

TECHNICAL REQUIREMENTS

One computer per group of 2–3 students, with an Internet connection and a Web browser.

PREPARATION

1 Find some Websites dealing with superstitions from English-speaking countries. Some suggestions for these can be found in Appendix E ('Activity links', page 121) or on our Website at *http://www.oup.com/elt/rbt.internet*

2 Prepare worksheets based on the model shown here.

PROCEDURE

1 Elicit some common superstitions, and their names in English. Ask whether the students think there is any logic behind them.

2 Discuss with them which of the superstitions they think are 'universal', and which they think are specific to their own culture. Give students the worksheets, and ask them to complete the first column with a list of superstitions from their own culture.

3 Send the students to the Websites you have chosen. Ask students to look at the Websites in their groups, and complete the worksheet with as much information as they can find.

4 The students present their findings to the rest of the class. The class add to their worksheets, noting those superstitions that are common to both cultures, and superstitions that exist only in one or the other.

5 Discuss the linguistic importance of talking about superstitions. (These are probably widely known in the target culture, and often have associated fixed expressions, so it is worth knowing about them.)

VARIATION 1   A search could be carried out on the Web to see how frequently some of these superstitions are referred to in documents.

VARIATION 2   This kind of activity can usefully be done as an email exchange with students in another country. Questions, answers, and information can be exchanged, or can be placed on a Web page.

Superstition in my culture	English equivalent (if any)	English superstition not found in my culture	Translation of English translation

Photocopiable © Oxford University Press

3.16 Knock, knock. Who's there?

LEVEL   Intermediate

TIME   30 minutes

AIMS   **To practise understanding and telling jokes in the target language.**

TECHNICAL REQUIREMENTS   One computer per group of 2–3 students, with an Internet connection and a Web browser.

PREPARATION   Choose one of the sites dedicated to jokes. Check the site for suitability of content and potential language problems. Suggestions for sites are included in Appendix E ('Activity links', page 121) or on our Website at *http://www.oup.com/elt/rbt.internet*

PROCEDURE

1 Ask the students to think of some jokes in their own language. Then ask them if they know any jokes in English. If they don't, put them into groups and get them to translate one joke into English.

2 Each group tells their joke (in English!) to the rest of the class.

3 Send the students to the joke Website you have chosen. Ask students to read the jokes to each other, and try to understand them. Students should make a note of any problems with vocabulary or comprehension, and choose a favourite joke.

4 Each group tells the rest of the class their favourite joke from the Web page.

5 Discuss any problems the students found.

FOLLOW-UP 1

If the site accepts submissions, students could write their own joke and submit it for publication.

FOLLOW-UP 2

Students could return to the Web page each week to build up a collection of favourite jokes in English.

3.17 All in the stars

LEVEL

Intermediate to advanced

TIME

30 minutes

AIMS

To practise the language of speculation and prediction.

TECHNICAL REQUIREMENTS

One computer per pair of students, with an Internet connection and a Web browser.

PREPARATION

Choose one of the Internet sites dedicated to fortune-telling. Suggestions for these can be found in Appendix E ('Activity links', page 121) or on our Website at *http://www.oup.com/elt/rbt.internet*

Check the site for potential vocabulary problems before the lesson.

PROCEDURE

1 Ask the students to write down three adjectives describing their personality, and three things they would like to do in future.

2 Revise relevant language, for example:

- *I am serious/hard-working/adventurous/reliable/exciting . . .*
- *I want to, I would (really) like/love to . . .*
- *One of my ambitions is to . . .*
- *One of my dreams is . . .*
- *I think/believe/hope/wish/ . . .*
- *It's possible/likely/unlikely that . . .*

3 Put the students in pairs and ask them to write down some adjectives to describe the other person's personality, and to make some predictions about what the other person might do, or what may happen to them in the future. Ask them to think of things that are likely, possible, and unlikely. Students should NOT show their partners what they have written yet.

4 Send students to the site you have chosen, and ask them to make notes about the predictions the site makes about them. Working in their pairs, they should discuss any difficult vocabulary or grammar.

5 Still in their pairs, students should compare the predictions with what they want or hope for themselves, and with the predictions they made for each other. They should make a note of predictions that are very close to their own, predictions that are very different from their own, and predictions that are very far-fetched, amusing, or interesting. They should also make a note of any new or difficult vocabulary.

6 Bring the whole class together to discuss their opinion of the site's predictions. How do they think the predictions are made? Ask how the site compares with other examples of fortune-telling that students may have come across, for example, in magazines, or with real-life fortune-tellers.

3.18 Desert Island Discs

LEVEL	**Upper-elementary and above**
TIME	**45 minutes**
AIMS	**To use the Internet as a source of materials to stimulate conversation; to talk about musical preferences.**
TECHNICAL REQUIREMENTS	One computer per group of 2–3 students, with an Internet connection and a Web browser.
KNOWLEDGE	Students should be competent at searching for information on the Internet.
PREPARATION	Find a Website with a set of biographies of famous people. Prepare a list of ten celebrities who are likely to be of interest to your students. Find two or three Websites with an appropriately eclectic collection of sound clips. For suggestions, see Appendix E ('Activity links', page 121) or our Website at *http://www.oup.com/elt/rbt.internet*

Choose a piece of music which relates to some period of your life, and which you will be happy to talk to students about. If possible, bring in the music to play to the students in class.

PROCEDURE

1 Tell the students about your chosen piece of music and explain why it is important to you. Play them the piece if you can.

2 Describe the *Desert Island Discs* programme on BBC Radio Four in the UK (see Note 1). Explain that it is one of the most popular and long-running programmes on radio. Ask them why they think this is. If possible, play them an extract from a recent programme.

3 Tell the students that they are going to put together their own mini *Desert Island Discs* programme from material on the Web. Ask them to predict the problems they might face.

4 Put students into groups of 2–3, and give them the list of celebrities you have prepared. Ask each group of students to pick a celebrity.

5 Send the groups to the celebrity Website, and ask them to locate and read their celebrity's biography. Ask students to note three events or sets of circumstances in the celebrity's life that they would associate with a particular type of music. Using one of the sound file sites, the students then locate suitable musical examples.

6 Re-group the students, so that each student in the new group has a different celebrity. Working from their notes, students interview each other in the style of *Desert Island Discs*.

7 Ask the students to think of a piece of music which has a strong connection with something that has happened in their lives. Ask them to talk about the music, and why it is important to them, in pairs.

NOTES

1 In *Desert Island Discs*, celebrities must imagine they are going to a desert island. They must choose eight pieces of music to take with them. They play the music, and explain the reasons for their choices to the programme presenter, who also asks all about their lives and careers.

2 As an alternative to visiting one of the many music sites, students could use a search engine to locate files in a suitable format. Many search engines allow searches by media type. See Appendix B3, 'Searching for information on the Web', page 107, for help with this.

3 More advanced classes could write up the interview, and save it, with the audio links to which it refers, on a Web page. Note that publishing audio files on a publicly available Website could contravene copyright law.

Integrated skills focus

3.19 Once upon a time

LEVEL	**Intermediate to advanced**
TIME	**45–90 minutes**
AIMS	**To practise reading and telling stories.**
TECHNICAL REQUIREMENTS	One computer per student or group of 2–3 students, with an Internet connection and a Web browser.
PREPARATION	Find at least one Website with traditional stories or folk tales from English-speaking countries. Suggestions for suitable sites can be found in Appendix E ('Activity links', page 121) or on our Website at *http://www.oup.com/elt/rbt.internet*

PROCEDURE

1 Ask the students to think of at least one story that is traditional in their culture. Write a list of titles on the board.

2 Ask them to work in groups and tell their stories in English.

3 Send students to the site(s) you have chosen. Ask them to look for a story which is similar to a traditional story from their own culture.

4 Next, students should try to find a story that is new to them. They should save this story.

5 Distribute the copied stories to all students in the class, either in printed form or on a **public drive**. Students look at all the stories. Have any of the students heard the stories before?

FOLLOW-UP

Ask the students to work through their story, trying to solve any language problems. They should bring any questions they still have about the story to the next class.

VARIATION 1

The students can be asked to write questions about their stories for other students in the class to answer. The stories and questions can then be put together as a collection to be used with that class and with others.

VARIATION 2

For more advanced students, the structure of the stories can be analysed, to see if traditional stories in English are told using the same structure as those in their own language.

VARIATION 3

This activity could be done using urban myths rather than traditional stories. The Internet, including email, is teeming with urban myths, often passed off as true stories!

3.20 Salute the flag

LEVEL

Intermediate

TIME

15–30 minutes

AIMS

To practise reading and talking about national flags and anthems; to practise describing visual patterns and images.

TECHNICAL REQUIREMENTS

One computer per student or group of 2–3 students, with an Internet connection and a Web browser.

PREPARATION

1 Find at least one Web page with images of national flags. Suggestions for suitable sites can be found in Appendix E ('Activity links', page 121) or on our Website at *http://www.oup.com/elt/rbt.internet*

2 Prepare a list of countries with distinctive flags. Prepare a worksheet, poster, or Website with numbered images of the flags on your list.

PROCEDURE

1 Elicit from the students some of the vocabulary necessary to describe national flags:

Colours, cross, circle, stars, stripes, . . .

2 Give each group the name of one of the countries from your list. Send them to the Website you have chosen, and ask them to find the flag for that country.

3 Students must decide how to describe their flag so that the rest of the class can recognize it from their description.

4 Show students the poster or Website you have prepared, or give them each a copy of the worksheet.

5 Ask each group to describe their flag. While they are doing so, the other students should write down the number of the flag that is being described.

6 When all of the groups have described their flag, ask them to confirm which flag they were describing.

7 Deal with any language points that occurred during the activity.

3.21 Coming to a theatre near you

LEVEL

Intermediate and above

TIME

60–90 minutes

AIMS

To practise note-taking and giving a short presentation.

TECHNICAL REQUIREMENTS

One computer per group of 2–3 students, with an Internet connection, a Web browser, and a word-processing program.

PREPARATION

1 Prepare a list of films which are shortly to be released in the country or region you are working in.

2 Find a Website, or Websites, giving details of the films. Appendix E ('Activity links', page 121) and our Website at *http://www.oup.com/elt/rbt.internet* give suggestions for these sites.

PROCEDURE

1 Explain that students are going to research forthcoming films, to see which one they would most like to see.

2 Give students the list of films you have prepared, and send them to the sites you have found. Ask each group to choose a different film to find out about.

3 Students read about their film and make notes in a word-processor file.

4 The students then edit their notes to form the basis of a presentation to the class.

5 The students give their presentations, trying to persuade the other students to see their film.

6 After all the presentations have been given, the class votes on which film(s) they would most like to see.

VARIATION 1

The notes that the students make for their presentation could be emailed to you, or to another group of students, for (peer) correction.

VARIATION 2

If the students or the school has its own **intranet** or Internet pages, they could put their notes into a 'forthcoming films' section. Updating this could become a regular project.

VARIATION 3

Students could go and see a film when it opens and write a review of it, comparing their opinion with the reviews they have read. In this way, a collection of class film reviews can be built up.

VARIATION 4

Similar activities can be done with other events taking place locally, such as concerts or plays.

Translation focus

3.22 Not so automatic

LEVEL	**Intermediate and above, with an interest in translation (but see variation for low-level students)**
TIME	**45–60 minutes**
AIMS	**To evaluate automatic translation.**
TECHNICAL REQUIREMENTS	One computer per group of 2–3 students, with an Internet connection, a Web browser, and a word-processing program.

PREPARATION

1 Familiarize yourself with the automatic translation features available on the Web. Suggestions for examples of these are included in Appendix E ('Activity links', page 121) and on our Website at *http://www.oup.com/elt/rbt.internet*

2 Choose a few English-language Web pages suitable for students to translate.

PROCEDURE

1 Divide the students into small groups. Give each group a Web page, and ask them to work together to translate it into their own language.

2 Help with vocabulary problems.

3 Elicit from the students what they have heard about automatic translation. Ask them to predict possible problems for automatic translation in the text they have just translated.

4 Tell students to use the automatic translation feature you have found to translate the Web page they have been working on.

5 The groups compare the two different translations and report their findings to the class.

VARIATION

Low-level students could be shown a Web page, in English, and asked to guess what the text might mean. They then use the automatic translation feature to translate the page into their own language, and evaluate the translation.

NOTES

This Activity is suitable for monolingual classes whose first language appears in automatic translation tools.

3.23 TranSearch

LEVEL	Elementary
TIME	15–30 minutes
AIMS	**To use the Internet to verify a translation.**
TECHNICAL REQUIREMENTS	One computer per student or group of 2–3 students, with an Internet connection and a Web browser.
KNOWLEDGE	Students should be familiar with searching for text on the Internet.
PREPARATION	Prepare some short English texts for the class to translate into their own language.

PROCEDURE

1 Give each group one of the texts to translate. Ask them to look through the text for phrases they find difficult. Tell students to attempt a translation of these phrases, using conventional reference tools such as dictionaries.

2 When the students have done their best to translate the phrases, ask them to go to an Internet search engine, and search for the original English phrases.

3 The students look at some of the hits they return, to learn more about the way their phrases are used in a variety of contexts.

4 The students then check and modify their translations, if necessary.

5 The groups present their new phrases to the rest of the class, along with their translations and the contexts in which they are used.

VARIATION

Students can be encouraged to perform this kind of check for all new, difficult phrases they encounter.

NOTES

1 This activity is suitable for monolingual classes.

2 The European Union's online translation database is a useful site for students to learn more about their suggested phrases. See Appendix E, page 121.

Acknowledgements

This activity was suggested to us by Paul Covill.

3.24 Cognitive translation

LEVEL	**Intermediate and above**
TIME	**60–90 minutes**
AIMS	**To practise translating news content.**
TECHNICAL REQUIREMENTS	One computer per student or per group of 2–3 students, with an Internet connection, Web browser, and a word-processing program.
PREPARATION	Find news stories which have been reported in both English-language online news sources, and on news Websites in the students' own language. Make sure that the English versions of the stories contain more detail than the versions in the students' first language. Suggestions for international online news resources can be found in Appendix E ('Activity links', page 121) or on our Website at *http://www.oup.com/elt/rbt.internet*

PROCEDURE

1 Ask the students what has been in the news recently. Introduce one of the stories that you have chosen.

2 Send the students to the pages you have found with the story in the students' first language and English.

3 Ask the students to find some pieces of information in the English-language report that are not in the report in their own language.

4 Tell the students to imagine that the news source from their country wishes to increase its coverage of the news event by 100 words. They have to decide which of the new information from the English-language article is the most important, and add it to the story in their own language.

5 Students paste the text of the story in their own language into the word-processor. They work together in their groups to extend the text.

6 Groups compare their new texts, and discuss any problems they encountered in carrying out the task.

VARIATION 1

The news story could be about an event which happened in the student's own country, and therefore requires the English text to be extended.

VARIATION 2

The activity could be done with just an English news item, with the students being asked to produce a version in their own language. If the students are asked to produce a version that is very different in length from the original, they will have to think carefully about the content rather than just produce a literal translation. If the new text is much shorter, the students are essentially using summarizing as well as translation skills.

NOTES

This activity is suitable for monolingual classes.

3.25 Made to measure

LEVEL	**Intermediate and above**
TIME	**90 minutes +**
AIMS	**To translate complete Web pages.**
TECHNICAL REQUIREMENTS	One computer per student, or per group of 2–3 students, with an Internet connection, a Web browser, and Web-authoring software or a word-processing program.
PREPARATION	This activity uses Web pages written about the students' institution in their first language. If there are no such pages, you could set the task of writing some as homework before the lesson.

PROCEDURE

1 Discuss with the class the benefits of having multilingual versions of their institution's Web pages.
2 Ask students to decide which parts of their institution's Website could be most usefully translated into English.
3 Ask students to consider the special problems of translating an entire Website, rather than a simple piece of text. They will have to consider space and design constraints, and make sure their translated text fits into the same space as the original.
4 Divide the students into groups, and assign each group to a part of the Website.
5 The students translate the pages, working in a Web-authoring or word-processing program to create new English-language versions of the complete pages. Give help where required.
6 When the task is finished, discuss any difficulties students had. Ask students what they have learnt about translation from doing this activity.

FOLLOW-UP

When the pages are finished, you can publish them on the institution's Website.

VARIATION

The students search for cultural organizations such as museums and galleries in their country which are on the Web, and which have information available only in their first language. They can then translate some of the institution's pages. They could also email the institution to offer the translated pages for publication.

NOTES

Because students must take space and design constraints into account, translating complete Web pages encourages them to translate the ideas in the original rather than just create a literal linguistic translation.

3.26 Simultaneous interpreters

LEVEL

Advanced

TIME

15–30 minutes

AIMS

To practise simultaneous interpretation.

TECHNICAL
REQUIREMENTS

One computer per student or group of 2–3 students, with an Internet connection, a Web browser, a sound card, and speakers. One machine will have to have speakers powerful enough for the audio to be heard by everyone in the room.

PREPARATION

Find a site which has long audio clips in English. Choose some which are suitable for simultaneous translation into the students' own language. The clips should not be part of a live broadcast, as students will want to pause the clip and listen again to check their work. Ideas for suitable sites can be found in Appendix E ('Activity links', page 121) or on our Website at *http://www.oup.com/elt/rbt.internet*

PROCEDURE

1 Ask the students if they have ever seen simultaneous interpreters at work. Tell them they are going to practise the skill of simultaneous interpretation, by listening to information in English and translating into their own language.

2 Choose a strong student, or preferably, ask for a volunteer, to demonstrate the activity.

3 Go to the site you have found and play the first audio clip. Ask the chosen student to begin the simultaneous translation. As the student speaks, adjust the volume of the original so both it and the student can be heard by the rest of the class.

4 Once the sound is balanced, get ready to start the activity with the whole class. Tell students that they must listen to the translation, and also watch for your signal. When you signal to a student, he or she should begin translating.

5 Start the audio clip. Change the student who is translating reasonably frequently.

6 Put the students into pairs or small groups to continue the activity with further audio clips. Point out that students can pause or rewind the clip if they are really stuck, but that the other members of their group should make sure they do not pause for too long.

VARIATION 1

If the students are not very strong at simultaneous interpretation, the transmission can frequently be paused, to allow the students more time to marshal their thoughts.

VARIATION 2   If students have microphones, they could actually record their work and exchange it.

VARIATION 3   If the students have to pass an interpretation examination, a live broadcast could also be used.

NOTES   Simultaneous interpretation is one of the most difficult language activities. The digital audio available on the Internet allows students to practise the skill with a large variety of easily controlled clips.

Appendices

Appendix A Glossary of Internet terms

Online Internet glossaries and explanations of computing terms in general are available online—see Appendix D2 (page 118).

applet

A small program written in the Java programming language. Some **Web** pages include applets, which run when the Web page opens.

ASCII

An ASCII file consists of plain text, without any formatting. ASCII is an acronym for American Standard Code for Information Interchange, and ASCII codes represent upper- and lower-case letters, numerals, and punctuation.

asynchronous

Not in 'real time'. Asynchronous communication takes place when a message sent by one person will not be received and answered immediately by the person it is sent to. **Email** is an example of asynchronous communication. Text, audio-, or video-conferencing are examples of **synchronous** communication, because messages are sent and received almost immediately, as in ordinary face-to-face communication.

attachment

A document which is sent along with an **email** message. It can be any type of computer file, including text, graphics, sound, or video.

bandwidth

The capacity of a network connection. The more bandwidth a network or **Internet** connection has, the faster the information will move along it. Connections with a high bandwidth are important for sending files containing graphics, sound, or video.

baud

The number of times a binary digit (bit) changes in a transmission medium per second. 56,000-baud is another way of saying 56,000 bits per second. The speed of a **modem** is usually described in terms of baud-rate, so a modem that has a speed of 56,000 baud (or 56 kb) will transfer information up to four times as fast as a 14,400-baud (or 14.4 kb) modem.

bookmarks

You can keep a record of a **Web** page that you visit in **Netscape** by 'bookmarking' the page. To visit that page again you can choose from your list of bookmarks rather than having to remember and type the **Web** page address (or **URL**). See also **favorites** and Chapter 1, pages 22–3.

browser

A program that allows you to read documents on the Web. **Netscape Navigator** and **Internet Explorer** are the most widely used, but others include **Mosaic**, Opera, and Lynx.

bulletin board system (BBS)	A bulletin board or message board is similar to a **newsgroup**, but instead of using **email**, users log on to the bulletin board Website to read and leave messages.
cache	A temporary storage area, either in the computer's memory or on disk, which allows previously used Web pages to be retrieved from a local store rather than from their original site, and therefore speeds up access.
CALL	Computer-Assisted Language Learning.
CGI	Common Gateway Interface. A method for running programs on a Web server based on input from a Web **browser**. A CGI script might allow a remote user access to a local database, for example, or to process the input of a multiple-choice test. See also **IRC**.
conferencing	**Synchronous** discussion via the Internet, using text, audio, or video. See Appendix C3, page 113, and C5, page 114.
cookie	Some Websites are designed to copy some information to your hard disk, often so that they can identify you when you visit that Website again. Such information is known as a 'cookie'. You can set your **browser** to accept or refuse 'cookies', though some Websites won't allow access unless you accept them.
decode	**Email** programs encode attachments before sending them, and decode them when they receive them. (See **attachment** and **encode**.)
discussion list	A public forum for discussion using **email**. Users send email to a computer, to be forwarded (usually automatically) to all subscribers to the list. Also known as a mailing list. See Appendix C2, page 112.
domain	The name given to the computer which links you to the Internet. It appears after the @ sign in an email address.
download	To copy something from another computer to your own. For example, Web pages, email messages, or software can be downloaded on to your computer. (See also **upload**.)
email	Electronic mail—a way of sending messages via the Internet (see Appendix C1, page 111).
emoticon	A symbol, or string of symbols, used to convey emotion in a text-only document, for example, :-) to indicate a smile, or the fact that a statement is not serious. Emoticons are sometimes called **smileys**.
encode	When you send an attachment with an email message, the email program will 'encode' it into a particular form in order to transmit it, and the email program that the recipient uses will have to 'decode' it. Common formats are MIME, Binhex, and Uuencode. Most recent versions of email software should encode and decode attachments successfully without the user having to worry about the process.
Explorer	See **Internet Explorer**.

FAQ	Frequently Asked Questions. A list of common questions relating to a newsgroup, a discussion list, or a similar service (see Appendix C2, page 112).
favorites	The **Internet Explorer** equivalent of **Bookmarks** in **Netscape**.
firewall	A set of programs running on a network gateway or **proxy server**, to protect users from outside interference.
flame	Noun: an inflammatory statement in an electronic-mail message. Verb: to send an angry message to a discussion list or **newsgroup**.
frame	Web pages can be divided into smaller, independent 'windows', or frames. Indexes can be created, for example, in a frame on the left hand side of the screen, which stays in position as the user moves from item to item in the main frame. Not all **browsers** can display frames.
FTP	File Transfer Protocol. A program for transferring files between computers. When Web pages are written, the author uses an FTP program to transfer the pages (the files) to the Web server.
GIF	Graphics Information File. One of the two standard formats (the other is **JPEG**) for displaying still graphics on a Web page.
HTML	HyperText Markup Language. Not really a language, but rather a set of tags which allows a **browser** to format and display a document. A page on the Web is an html document because it is formatted with html tags.
HTTP	Hyper Text Transfer Protocol. The instructions which allow a **hypertext** document to be transmitted over the **World Wide Web**. **http://** will usually be found at the beginning of a Web page address (or **URL**).
hypertext	Text which can be read in a non-linear way. Hypertext is text in which links have been inserted to allow the reader to jump to a different part of the document.
ICT	Information and Communications Technology. An increasingly common term in Europe for what used to be called 'IT': Information Technology.
Internet	A network linking computers around the globe. The **Web** is a medium for presenting information on the Internet. **Email** is transmitted through the Internet.
Internet Explorer	A **World Wide Web browser**.
Internet Relay Chat	See **IRC**.
intranet	A local network which runs software, such as a Web browser, to present information to people working within a particular organization, rather than making it publicly available via the Internet. See also **LAN**.
IP	Internet Protocol. The instructions which control the passage of packets of data around the Internet. A computer which you use when you are connected to the Internet will have an IP address to identify it.

IRC   Internet Relay Chat. Software which allows a number of Internet
                         users to connect and 'converse' in real time. A message typed by
                         one user will appear at the same time on the screens of all of the
                         other users taking part in the 'chat'. This is an example of
                         synchronous communication. See Appendix C3, page 113.

ISDN   Integrated Services Digital Network. A telecommunications
                         technology allowing transmission speeds significantly faster than
                         those available through a **modem**. ISDN lines carry any kind of
                         data, including voice.

JANET   The UK academic and research network. An acronym for Joint
                         Academic Network.

JPEG   Joint Picture Expert Group. A standard format for the
                         compression of still pictures on the Web. See also **GIF**.

keypals   Computer penpals.

LAN   Local Area Network: a computer network limited to an immediate
                         area.

LISTSERV   A general term for email-based **discussion lists**. More accurately,
                         the name of one particular program for organizing and
                         maintaining discussion lists.

lurking   Just listening to the discussion on a **discussion list** or
                         newsgroup, without actively participating.

modem   (from MODulator, DEModulator) A piece of equipment that
                         allows a computer to send information to, and to receive
                         information from, other computers, through a telephone line.

MOO   'Multi-user domain, Object-Oriented'. Software which allows
                         multiple users to interact in an imaginary environment, usually by
                         typing in information at the keyboard. See Appendix C4, page
                         113.

Mosaic   A **World Wide Web browser** created by the National Center for
                         Supercomputer Applications.

MUD   A Multi-User Domain. Software which allows multiple users to
                         interact in a computer-generated environment. See also **MOO**.

netiquette   Computer etiquette. A set of conventions for polite behaviour on
                         the Internet. Less trivial than it sounds.

Netscape (Navigator)   A **World Wide Web browser**.

newsgroup   A discussion group whose proceedings are hosted on **Usenet**.

plugin   A piece of software used within a **browser** which automatically
                         handles a **remote** file (often multimedia) without the user's
                         intervention. Well-known plugins include RealPlayer, Shockwave,
                         and Flash.

portal   A site which provides a 'gateway' into a range of Web services.
                         Portals generally combine Web search facilities with a directory of
                         listings, organized by category. Well-known portal sites include
                         Yahoo! and AltaVista.

proxy server	A server which acts as an intermediary between the user and the Internet. It often has a security function (i.e. to keep out unwanted visitors) and holds a cache for all network users.
public drive	On a local area network (**LAN**), a public drive allows users to both read files from it and save files to it. Also known as **shared drive**.
remote	In a different place. A file which is saved on your own computer is a local file. A file held on another computer is a remote file.
search engine	A program which allows a user to search for specific information, usually by matching the search words with their occurrence on Web pages. There are over twenty engines on the Web, all operating in slightly different ways, and with varying speed and reliability. Among the most popular are AltaVista, Lycos, and Excite.
server	A computer or a piece of software that provides a resource to other computers on a network. For example, the Web pages for a particular Website will usually be kept on a single computer known as the **Web server**.
shared drive	See **public drive**.
smiley	See **emoticon**.
SP	Service Provider. A company which provides Internet services (and therefore often called an ISP) to the general public. Well-known SPs include CompuServe, AOL, and, in the UK, Pipex, Demon, and Freeserve. See Appendix D2 for service providers' **URL**s.
spamming	Sending the same email to multiple lists, newsgroups, or individuals, usually to advertise a product or service. Viewed as a serious breach of **netiquette**.
stop list	A list of common words ('the', 'a', 'and', etc.) which are excluded from searches made by a search engine or database.
surfing	The verb which is usually used to describe the process of moving from page to page and site to site on the Web. Given the speed at which the Web sometimes operates, it is difficult to see why this particular verb was chosen.
synchronous	Text, audio-, or video-conferencing are examples of synchronous communication: messages are sent and received almost immediately, as in ordinary face-to-face communication. See also **asynchronous**.
Telnet	A type of software which allows a computer to log on to a **remote** computer and work as if it were directly attached to that computer. Used to access **MOO**s, Gopher, Archie, and other Internet resources.
UNIX	An operating system used by the majority of service providers on the Internet, originally developed at AT&T Bell Labs but now an 'open', non-proprietary system.
upload	To copy a file from your own to another computer. For example, if you write a Web page, to make it available on the Web you will

usually have to upload it to another computer which acts as the Web server. See also **download**.

URL   Uniform Resource Locator. The unique address which indicates the location of a page of information on the World Wide Web, for example: *http://www.britcoun.org*

Usenet   A collection of over 18,000 informally linked **newsgroups** for specialized discussions. Sometimes called 'Network News'.

WAIS   Wide Area Information Service—information that is made available over a wide area, using a network such as the Internet.

Web   See **World Wide Web**.

whiteboarding   Some Internet conferencing programs provide a 'whiteboard', allowing participants to put pictures and text on the screen which can be seen and worked on by all participants in the conference.

World Wide Web   Sometimes known as the WorldWideWeb, or increasingly as just the Web. This is a means of making information available over the Internet, using a standard way of formatting text. See **HTML**.

Appendix B The Web

B1 Surfing the Web

Moving from Web page to Web page or Website to Website, or navigating around the Web, is commonly known as surfing. This, however, gives an impression of speed, which is often unjustified. If your Internet connection works slowly and Web pages take a long time to download, there are a number of simple things you can do to speed the process up:

1 Do things in parallel

Two windows are better than one
If you want to visit more than one Web site, you can save time by downloading pages from more than one Website at a time. Just open two copies of your Web browser and download pages from different Websites on each of them.

When you follow a link on a Web page, you can open the link in a separate window. It will then be quicker to return to the page with the original link as it is, still open. To do this on a Windows computer, right-click on the link then choose *Open in new window;* on a Mac, hold the button down until the menu appears.

2 Switch things off

Text and images
Images on Web pages are often decorative rather than essential and Web pages sometimes offer text-only versions which you can choose. These will load much more quickly than pages with graphics. Alternatively, you can switch off the automatic loading of images, and pages will then download much more quickly. This can be done in the Edit Preference settings of Netscape, and in the Internet Options: Advanced settings of Explorer. If you want to see images on a particular page, you can always switch on the loading of images again and reload the page.

Javascript
Some Web pages are designed to open an extra 'pop-up' window automatically when they are downloaded. These extra windows take time to download and often contain unimportant messages or advertisements. They can usually be avoided by disabling Javascript in the Edit Preference settings of Netscape, and in the Internet Options: Advanced settings of Explorer. If you decide you want to allow Javascript to run on a particular page, you can always enable it again and reload the page.

'Cookies'
Web sites often want to download 'cookies' onto your hard disk.

These are sometimes claimed to speed up Web pages, but often
they just send information about you back to the Website. They
take time to download, and if you set your browser so that it asks
you if you want to accept 'cookies', you have to spend time
responding to these requests. You can switch cookies off in
Netscape Preferences or Internet Explorer Options. Some
Websites require you to accept 'cookies', but for these sites you
can always switch them on again and reload the page.

Advertisements

Pages often display advertisements that you don't want to see, but
which take a long time to download. You can sometimes stop
these by selecting an option to stop animations loading. There are
also programs that allow you to filter out advertisements and
various other features, for example, Intermute (see Appendix D3,
page 119, for software Websites).

3 Save things

Hard disks and proxy servers

If you regularly use pages that don't change very often, it can be
worth saving them on your hard disk (see Appendix B2, 'Working
offline', below).

In addition, if your Internet Service Provider uses a **proxy server**,
frequently-accessed pages may be saved there. They will usually
then download much more quickly than if you have to go to the
original site. Your ISP will provide details of how to access their
proxy server.

B2 Working offline

Many packages exist which allow you to copy pages and work
offline. Some popular ones are listed in Appendix D3, with Web
addresses.

In addition, Netscape Communicator allows you to save
individual pages, including all graphics on them, by choosing
File:Edit Page or Edit Frame, and Internet Explorer allows you to
copy single pages and whole sites for offline browsing. For the
latest information on what is available, and to download
demonstration software, go to the Tucows site (see Appendix D3)
and find the 'Offline Browsers' section.

Offline browsers will normally allow you to copy either single
pages (including their graphics) or complete sites. Care needs to
be exercised: it is very easy to fill your hard disk completely by
copying a single, large site! Copying text and graphics is not
usually a problem, but multimedia elements can be difficult,
although offline browsers are constantly being rewritten to keep up

with changing technology, and can handle some of the more popular formats (Shockwave, for example). Any interactive pages, however, such as those which ask you to fill in a questionnaire or complete a multiple-choice test, cannot be copied satisfactorily.

As well as copying the pages, the software will rename them and adjust the links, so that the connection between pages can be retained. This is not always successful, and may require you to make some of the links manually (assuming that you know how to!).

B3   Searching for information on the Web

Search engines vary in their features and how they are implemented. AltaVista is used here as an example. See Appendix E, page 121, for more examples, or our Website *http//www.oup.com/elt/rbt.internet*

Constructing a query using AltaVista

AltaVista is a powerful search engine. It does not index as many pages as some search engines, but it is fast and reliable. Here are some tips for getting the best out of it.

Simple searches

AltaVista has two modes of use: simple and 'advanced text search'. Simple is enough for most queries.

Entering a query

1 You *can* just type in a word and hit *Submit*, but this is not recommended. Searching for *"China"*, for example, will produce over 4,000,000 documents which contain the word. Unless you are looking for something very unusual, you will normally need more than one search term.

2 Use + when a match is required, and – when it is prohibited. For example, if you were looking for pages about cod fishing, you might want to exclude fish and chip shops, by entering:

    +fishing +cod –chips

3 It is easy to miss the different forms of words: use * where appropriate. For example:

    +teach*

matches pages that contain at least one word such as teach, teacher, teaching.

We could improve our search for cod fishing by entering:

    +cod +fish*

4   Link words into a phrase with quotation marks.

5   Use lower-case as far as possible. Lower-case search will find matches of capitalized words also. For example, *student* will find matches for student, Student, and STUDENT. *Capital letters in a search will force an exact case match on the entire word.*

Constraining searches

It is possible to restrict searches by 'metatags'. The keyword should be in lower-case, and immediately followed by a colon. AltaVista has a whole range of metatags. Three of the most useful are title, **domain**, and **URL**.

title:Charles   Matches pages with the word 'Charles' in the title (e.g. Prince Charles). (The title is in the blue bar which appears at the top of each Web page.)

domain:uk   Matches pages according to where they originate. There are codes for type of business (*.com*, *.edu*, *.net*) and country codes (for example, *.uk* is for United Kingdom, *.hk* Hong Kong, etc.).

Image:tom   Matches pages which have an image in them called 'Tom'.

B4   Writing Web pages

The software

It can be as easy to write a Web page as to word-process a document. In fact, current versions of most word-processors should allow you to save a document in .htm or .html format, which will allow your page to be read using a Web browser. However, this is not the only way to write a Web page. There are six main tools you can use:

1   any word-processor or text-processor (such as Windows Notepad): type in the **HTML** codes yourself, and then save the page with the extension *.htm* or *.html*

2   an HTML editor (such as HotDog or Arachnophilia) which allows you to insert the HTML codes by choosing from menus

3   an older version of a word-processor, together with a conversion program (see Appendix D3)

4   a more recent version of a word-processor like Word (from Word 6 on); save the page in *.htm* or *.html* rather than *.doc* format

5   the editor that comes with your Web browser (for example, Netscape Composer)

6   a dedicated WYSIYG Web editor (like Frontpage or HotMetal) which allows you to type your Web page as if you were typing into a word-processor. These programs usually allow you to insert more features into your page than a word-processor, and

the more powerful ones also help you to manage other people's Web pages, or a whole Website.

4 and **5** are by far the easiest if you are teaching students to write their own Web pages. **1** and **2** are less difficult than they sound, but are only really necessary if you want greater control over the appearance and performance of the Web pages you write. Although it isn't difficult to learn HTML codes, most teachers and students are unlikely to want to spend the time doing so. **6** can be as easy as **4** and **5**, but such programs can also be very powerful and more difficult to learn.

Content

1 There should be a reason for the students to write their Web pages. Just as with any other document, the style and content of the Web pages will depend on the purpose and the audience it is intended for. Who is the audience? Is the page going to be displayed on a local area network, so that the audience is restricted and predictable, or is it going to be displayed on the Web, so that anyone can see it? Reasons for writing Web pages might include:

   • writing personal Web pages as part of an email exchange;

   • displaying information about a hobby or a class project;

   • writing academic papers, to be advertised on discussion lists, asking for feedback.

2 The students should think not only about the people who are going to read their pages, but about the equipment their readers might be using. Will their readers have any difficulty downloading Web pages with lots of pictures, sound, or even video? Will they have trouble reading different fonts and so on?

3 Do you want people who read the Web pages to be able to contact the students directly? If so, they should put their own email addresses on the Web pages if they have them. If you want first contacts to be channelled through you, then put your email address, or an institutional one, on the Web pages.

B5 Putting pages on the Web

If Web pages are to be displayed on an intranet (or a Local Area Network), they will usually just have to be copied on to a **public drive** on the network using Windows Explorer, File Manager, or the Desktop. Don't forget to keep a backup, and to tell the students to keep backup copies of their own, especially if other people have read and write access to the drive. If there is no drive that can be written to as well as read from by all users, you will need the network manager either to **upload** the pages for you, or to give you rights that will allow you to upload the pages yourself. This is more time-consuming than getting the students to upload pages by themselves, of course.

If Web pages are to be displayed on the Web, then the possibilities are the same as for Web pages that are to be displayed on a Local Area Network. Uploading the files may simply be a case of copying the files across using the Desktop on a Mac, File Manager, or Windows Explorer. However, you may have to use a File Transfer Protocol (FTP) program to do this if you are transferring to a Web server that runs Unix (CuteFTP works in a similar way to File Manager or Windows Explorer). Alternatively, programs like FrontPage or Netscape Composer allow you to send your pages directly from the program to the Web server.

One point to watch out for is that if your file server is a Unix machine, Unix is case-dependent, so your links may not work if you have not been careful to make sure that the name of the files you link to are in exactly the same case as the names in your links. Some editors automatically change the names of files to upper-case when they are copied over to a Unix file-server, but they don't change the names in the documents themselves. This is a common cause of links failing to work once the pages have been transferred to the Web server.

Your Internet Service Provider (ISP—the company that provides your connection to the Internet) will have space you can use for Web pages. There are many ISPs that offer free space for Web pages—see Appendix D2, page 118, for addresses.

If your students produce a large number of Web pages, your task will begin to involve managing a Website rather than just a collection of Web pages. Software such as FrontPage and Dreamweaver can help in producing and managing a Website as well in authoring Web pages, and there are books on managing Websites which you can consult (see the Bibliography on page 132).

The information contained in Appendix B was correct at the time of going to press, but may change. Please see our Website on *http//www.oup.com/elt/rbt.internet* for updates.

Appendix C Using computers for communication

As well as a source of information, computers are becoming increasingly important as a medium of communication, with distance education making use of Computer-Mediated Communication (CMC) techniques, and face-to-face education using Computer Managed Learning (CML) techniques.

C1   Email

As well as the basics of sending and reading messages, it is useful to learn how to do the following:

- **Send and receive attachments**. These are files that can be attached to email messages. Attachments can be text, graphics, or even audio or video files, but usually they will be word-processed documents, and using attachments is a good way of getting your students to submit written work to you, to be marked and commented on using a word-processor, and returned to the student as an email attachment.

- **Make mail folders and filter incoming mail into different folders**. If you receive a lot of email it can be very difficult to manage. Setting up filters so that different kinds of messages are automatically filtered off to particular folders is a useful technique for easing your workload. For example, if your learners submit work by email, if they put the subject as Homework in their message, you can filter all of the homework submitted by email into a separate Homework folder.

- **Set up address lists**. If you want to send the same message to a group of people—for example, to all of the students in a particular class—setting up address lists will allow you to send out the same message to all of the people in a particular address list at the same time by typing in just one address.

The exact details of using attachments, filters, and address lists will differ from email program to email program.

Free email addresses

There are many Websites that offer free email addresses. The list of such sites is constantly growing; a few of the best known, which include Hotmail, Eudoramail, and Yahoo, are listed in Appendix D2.

Most sites will allow you to set up more than one email address, which means that you can, for example, use a different address for mail you send to different people or organizations. You can also choose an email address that allows you to remain anonymous. All of this can be helpful in, for example, avoiding unwanted **spam** email.

C2   Discussion lists

Discussion lists are simply email systems where every email you send is copied automatically to all other subscribers. Most lists were originally run from mainframe or minicomputers at universities around the world, and many still are; but an increasing number are run from PCs or via the World Wide Web. You can start your own list by visiting one of the Web's most popular sites, Egroups. See Appendix D1, page 115, for a list of discussion groups and their addresses.

Most lists are free and can be joined or left any time. The method of subscription varies. Some can be joined simply by going to a Web page and filling in the appropriate form (see, for example, the British Council lists). Most, however, involve sending an email message to a computer address. For the most common list software, LISTSERV, you just send an email with the following in the body of your text:

SUB <Listname> <YourName>

So, if your name were Marie Curie, and you wanted to subscribe to TESL-L, you would write:

SUB TESL-L Marie Curie

Other lists may require different syntax. If you are not sure how to subscribe, just experiment. If you make a mistake, the list computer should send an explanatory message or detailed instructions.

Many people join a discussion list and just read other people's contributions without emailing, or posting, a message to the list themselves. This is known as **lurking** (on many lists a majority of members are probably lurkers or at least start as lurkers). If you lose your temper and send an angry message to a discussion list, this is known as **flaming.** Flaming is often the result of a misunderstanding, and to try to avoid comments in email messages being misunderstood, people often use **smileys** or **emoticons** like : -) or ; -) to show when they are not being serious. Flaming is bad **netiquette** (email etiquette).

Student lists

LaTrobe University in Australia runs lists for student use. These often have an advantage over conventional one-to-one or group-to-group email projects, in that there is almost always some sort of response. See Appendix D1 for a contact email address.

More information on student lists is to be found in Appendix E, Activity 1.9 (page 124).

More information

For up-to-date information on what lists are available and how to subscribe to them, see the list in Appendix D1 and on our Website *http//www.oup.com/elt/rbt.internet*

C3   Text-conferencing: Internet Relay Chat

If you use email, there is always a delay between your message being sent out, arriving at its destination, and a reply being sent and arriving on your computer. Text-conferencing software, however, is rather like immediate email as your message arrives on the other person's screen almost as soon as you send it, and the other person's reply will appear on your screen immediately he or she sends it. Internet Relay Chat (IRC) is the most common form of text-conferencing software, and this allows two or more people to have a text 'chat'. There are many sites around the world that host public 'chats' that anyone can join. It is also possible to set up 'chats' that only people you invite can join.

Unfortunately, the more people join in a 'chat', the more disjointed the discussion is. In addition, the contributions to the discussion are often short and people tend to use abbreviations, and make a lot of typing mistakes. Nevertheless, anyone can set up a 'chat room' (or 'chat group'), and IRC can be useful for discussion among a small number of people, especially as the discussion can be 'logged', i.e. a copy can be saved on disk, to look at more carefully later. It can be especially good at establishing contact with people, and 'breaking the ice'.

The most popular IRC program is *mIRC*, which can be found and downloaded from a number of places on the Web (see Appendix D2). It is quite easy to install. Other IRC software includes ICQ and Microsoft Chat.

C4   MOOs

'Chat rooms' set up using IRC software disappear once the participants have all logged out, and have to be set up again each time people want to 'chat'. MOOs (Multi-user domain, Object-Oriented), however, are like 'chat rooms' which don't disappear. As a result, people can join a MOO, choose a character, keep that character each time they take part in a discussion, give their character characteristics that others can read about, and store pre-fabricated bits of text which they can call up with just a few key-strokes. This makes it easier to take part in discussions, because phrases they use regularly don't have to be typed out in full.

MOOs are usually 'moderated', so that the owner of the MOO can decide who should and should not be allowed to join a group. This allows MOOs to make sure that participants all have similar interests and backgrounds, for example, so that discussions can be more focused. The most popular MOO for language teachers (though learners can participate as well) is schMOOze University (see Appendix D1 for the Internet address).

It is useful to know something about how to work in MOOs, and very important to be reasonably confident yourself if you are going to take students for a discussion there.

C5   Audio- and video-conferencing

Audio-**conferencing** is now becoming reasonably practical with current **modem** speeds. As with text-conferencing, it works best with a small number of participants. Video-conferencing can work acceptably using cameras with cards fitted in the computer. As computers have access to more and more **bandwidth**, audio- and video-conferencing is likely to increase in use.

C6   Bulletin board systems

Bulletin boards can be used to post messages to a group rather than emailing messages to each member. Bulletin boards have the advantage that all messages posted on the board are kept for users to refer to, and the messages are usually 'threaded' (the first message on a particular topic is kept together with subsequent messages on the same topic, so it is easy to follow the 'thread' of the discussion). They have the disadvantage that, to find out if any new messages have been posted, users have to go to the trouble of logging on to the site where the messages are kept, rather than having the messages sent to them automatically. Bulletin boards can be set up at Be Seen—see Appendix D2.

Appendix D Internet resources

We include here just a brief selection of addresses and links.

These links have been updated for the second impression of this book, and were correct at the time of going to press. As we have stressed before, the Internet is dynamic and changeable, and we recommend that you visit our Website *http://www.oup.com/elt/rbt. internet* which is regularly updated. We also welcome readers' feedback and suggestions.

Inclusion in these lists does not necessarily mean that the authors or publishers of this book endorse these sites or their content.

D1 English Language Teaching resources

Organizations

British Council	10 Spring Gardens, London SW1A 2BN, UK Tel: +44 (0)207 930 8466	*http://www.britcoun.org*
CALICO	The Computer Assisted Language Instruction Consortium, Duke University, 014 Language Center, Box 90267, Durham, NC 27708-0267, USA. Tel: +1 919 660 3180	*http://calico.org*
CILT	Centre for Information on Language Teaching and Research, 20 Bedfordbury, London WC2N 4LB, UK. Tel: +44 (0)207 379 5101 or 207 379 5110	*http://www.cilt.org.uk*
Computers in Teaching Initiative	Computers in Teaching Initiative, Centre for Modern Languages, School of European Languages, The University of Hull, Hull HU6 7RX, UK. Tel +44 (0)1482 465991 (Contact: June Thompson)	*http://www.hull.ac.uk/cti*
EuroCALL	CTI Centre for Modern Languages, University of Hull, Hull HU6 7RX, UK. Tel: +44 (0)1482 465872	*http://www.hull.ac.uk/cti/ eurocall.htm*
IATEFL: Computer Special Interest Group	IATEFL, 3 Kingsdown Chambers, Kingsdown Park, Tankerton, Whitstable, Kent CT5 2DJ, UK. Tel: +44 (0)1227 274415	*http://www.iatefl.org*

| TESOL: CALL Interest Section | Teachers of English to Speakers of Other Languages, Inc., 1600 Cameron Street, Suite 300, Alexandria, Virginia, 22314-2751, USA. Tel: +1 703 836 0774 | *http://www.tesol.edu* |

Email discussion lists

Lists for teachers

Egroups		*http://www.egroups.com*
British Council lists		*http://mis.britcoun.org*
APPLIX	Applied linguistics	*Majordomo@cltr.uq.oz.au*
COMP-SIG	IATEFL CALL SIG	Send an email message to: *Laurent.Borgmann@sk. fh-fulda.de* (IATEFL Members only)
DEOS-L	Distance Education	*Listserv@psuvm.psu.edu*
EST-L	English for Science and Technology	*Listserv@asuvm.inre.asu.edu*
JALTCALL	Japanese Association of Language Teachers	*Majordomo@clc.hyper. chubu.ac.jp*
LINGUIST	Applied Linguistics	*Listserv@tamvm1.tamu.edu*
NETEACH-L	Teaching ESL/EFL on the Net	*listserv@raven.cc.ukans.edu*
SLART-L	Second Language Acquisition	*listserv@cunyvm.cuny.edu*
TESL-L	General ESL/EFL	*listserv@cunyvm.cuny.edu*

Student lists

LaTrobe University	Send a blank e-mail message to *announce-sl @latrobe.edu.au*

For up-to-date information on what lists are available and how to subscribe to them, see the following Websites:

Tile.Net	*http://tile.net*
Liszt mailing list directory	*http://www.liszt.com*
Inter-Links	*http://alabanza.com/ kabacoff/Inter-Links/listserv. html*

MOOs

---

schMOOze University	*http://schmooze.hunter.cuny. edu:8888/*
Useful information about schMOOze can be found at:	*http://members.tripod.co.jp/ schmooze/*

Online teaching resources

Dave Sperling's ESL Cafe		*http://www.eslcafe.com/*
Digital Education Network	PO Box 322, Bedford MK44 2ZS, UK. Tel: +44 (0)1234 708946	*http://www.go-ed.com*
The Linguistic Funland TESL Page		*http://www.linguistic-funland. com/tesl.html*

Software publishers

Camsoft	10 Wheatfield Close, Maidenhead, Berks SL6 3PS, UK. (contact: Graham Davies) Tel: +44 (0)1628 825206	*http://ourworld.compuserve. com/homepages/ GrahamDavies1/homepage. htm*
Oxford University Press	Great Clarendon Street, Oxford OX2 6DP, UK Tel: +44 (0)1865 556767	*http://www.oup.com/elt*
Wida Software		*http://www.wida.co.uk/*

Online journals

An increasing number of journals are being published on the Web, and the following deal mainly with the use of technology, and especially computers, for language learning and teaching.

CALL Journal (Swets)	Abstracts only	*http://www.swets.nl/sps/ journals/call.html*
CALL Review (IATEFL)	Selected articles online	*http://www.iatefl.org/callsig/ callsig.htm*
The Internet TESL Journal		*http://www.aitech.ac.jp/~iteslj/*
Journal of Language Learning Technologies (IALL)	Some back issues online	*http://iall.net/iallj.html*
Language Learning & Technology	Fully online	*http://llt.msu.edu*
CALL-EJ Online	In 1999, *CALL-EJ*, a refereed journal edited by Kazunori Nozawa in Japan, joined *On-CALL Online* in Australia with a view to sharing resources and expertise. The name of the new collaborative journal is *CALL-EJ Online*. This collaboration aims to broaden and strengthen the base of CALL in	

	the Western Pacific area. The URL of the new journal is	*http://www.lerc.ritsumei.ac. jp/callej/index.html*
	OnCALL archive	*http://www.cltr.uq.edu.au/ oncall/*
ReCALL (CTI Modern Languages & EUROCALL)	Information, tables of contents and some back issues online	*http://www.hull.ac.uk/cti/ eurcall/recall.htm*

D2   Internet services

Internet Service Providers

| | For a full listing for the UK, see | *http://www.limitless.co.uk/ inetuk/providers.html* |

Software publishers

HomePage.com	130 W. Union St., Pasadena, CA 91103, USA	*http://www.homepage.com/*
Geocities (Yahoo)		*http://geocities.yahoo.com/ home/*
Tripod (Lycos)		*http://www.tripod.lycos.com/*
Be Seen		*http://www.beseen.com/*

Free email addresses

Hotmail		*http://www.hotmail.com*
Yahoo		*http://www.yahoo.com*
Eudora		*http://www.eudoramail.com*

Internet Relay Chat

| mIRC | | *http://www.mirc.co.uk/get.html* |

Bulletin board systems

| Be Seen | | *http://www.beseen.com/ board/index.html* |

Online Internet glossaries

| | | *http://seamonkey.ed.asu.edu/ ~storslee/terms.html* *http://www.matisse.net/files/ glossary.html* |
| computing terms in general | | *http://whatis.com* |

D3 Software

General

Cnet Download	*http://download.cnet.com/*
Cnet Shareware	*http://shareware.cnet.com/*
Tucows	*http://www.tucows.com*

Web browsers

Netscape Communicator	*http://home.netscape.com/*
Microsoft Internet Explorer	*http://www.microsoft.com/*
Opera	*http://www.operasoftware.com/*

Web editors

Arachnophilia	*http://www.arachnoid.com/*
Dreamweaver	*http://www.macromedia.com/*
HotDog	*http://www.sausage.com/*
Microsoft Frontpage	*http://www.microsoft.com/*
PageMill	*http://www.adobe.com*
Softquad HotMetal	*http://www.sq.com/*

Language authoring software

Half-Baked Software's Hot Potatoes	*http://wcb.uvic.ca/hrd/ halfbaked/*
	http://www.cict.co.uk/

FTP software

CuteFTP	*http://www.cuteftp.com*

Software for controlling access to Web sites

Software that blocks access

Cyber Patrol	The Learning Company, Cambridge, Mass, USA	*http://www.cyberpatrol.com*
CYBERsitter	99 Solid Oak Software, Santa Barbara, CA, USA	*http://www.cybersitter.com*
Net Nanny	Net Nanny Software, Vancouver, BC, Canada	*http://www.netnanny.com*
SafetyNet	Web Grip, Vancouver, WA, USA	*http://www.sitecensor.com*

Jansma, Nic	WatchDog, Grand Rapids, MO, USA	http://www.sarna.net/watchdog/
We-Blocker		http://www.we-blocker.com

Software that records access

FamilyCAM	Silverstone Software, Pittsburgh, USA	http://www.silverstone.net
Kid Control		http://www.kidcontrol.com/
Prudence	The Blue Wolf Network, Portland, OR, USA	http://www.bluewolfnet.com
Spector	SpectorSoft, Vero Beach, Florida, USA	http://www.spectorsoft.com
Surfing Spy	ESM Software	http://ourworld.compuserve.com/homepages/esmsoftware/sspy.htm
WinGuardian	Webroot Inc, Boulder, CO, USA	http://www.webroot.com

Programs which allow you to filter out advertisements

InterMute		http://www.adsubtract.com/im/

Software to copy Web pages and work offline

WebWhacker		http://www.bluesquirrel.com
WebZip		http://www.spidersoft.com
Tucows		http://www.tucows.com

To convert word-processing files to HyperText

EasyHTML		http://www.easyhtml.com/

Appendix E Activity links

This section contains suggested Websites for the Activities in
Chapters 1, 2, and 3.

These links were correct at the time of going to press, but as we
have stressed before, the Web is dynamic and changeable. Please
see our Website at *http//www.oup.com./elt/rbt.internet* for updates
and further links.

| **1.1** | **It all depends** |
| **1.2** | **Desperately seeking …** |

Search engines

AltaVista	*http://www.altavista.com*
Northern Light	*http://www.northernlight.com*
Hotbot	*http://www.hotbot.com*

| **1.3** | **Starspotting** |

Search engines

AltaVista	*http://www.altavista.com*
Northern Light	*http://www.northernlight.com*
Excite	*http://www.excite.com*

Category-based Web directories

Yahoo!	*http://www.yahoo.com*
Excite	*http://www.excite.com*
AltaVista	*http://www.altavista.com*

| **1.4** | **Where did I put it?** |

*The following are example sites which could be classified in various
ways under headings such as: news, travel, music, shopping,
newspapers, radio/TV, media.*

Broadcast.com	*http://www.broadcast.com*
BBC News	*http://news.bbc.co.uk*
British Tourist Authority	*http://www.visitbritain.com*
CD Universe	*http://www.cduniverse.com*
Mr Showbiz	*http://mrshowbiz.go.com*
CNN Interactive	*http://www.cnn.com*
Electronic Telegraph	*http://www.telegraph.co.uk*
FOX News	*http://foxnews.com*
Rough guides to travel	*http://travel.roughguides.com*

SonicNet: The Online Music Network	*http://www.sonicnet.com*
Guardian Unlimited	*http://www.guardian.co.uk*
Yalplay (The Interactive Music & Video Shop)	*http://www.boxman.com*
The International Lyrics Server	*http://songfile.snap.com/index_2. html*
The Sydney Morning Herald	*http://www.smh.com.au*
The Times Internet Edition	*http://www.the-times.co.uk*
Travelfinders	*http://www.travelfinders.com*
The Washington Post	*http://www.washingtonpost.com*

Evaluating Web pages

There are many sites on the Web with information about how Web pages can be evaluated.

An Internet quiz

The following site has a quiz that tests people's expectations about the Web.

| Internet/Internot Quiz: | *http://www.gvsu.edu/library/intnotqz.htm* |

Evaluating the design and appearance of Web pages

The following Web pages have information about designing and judging the design of Web pages:

http://info.med.yale.edu/caim/manual/ pages/page_design.html

Evaluating the status of Web pages

The following Web pages have information about judging the status of information on the Web:

http://www2.widener.edu/Wolfgram-Memorial-Library/webeval/eval1198/ index.htm

http://www.gvsu.edu/library/Evaluating. htm

http://www.tiac.net/users/hope/ findqual.html

http://longman.awl.com/englishpages/ citation.htm

http://www.vanguard.edu/rharris/ evalu8it.htm
and
http://school.discovery.com/schrockguide/ eval.html (this site is particularly aimed at primary and secondary school teachers)

1.5 And the award goes to...

The following addresses offer listings of 'cool sites'

The Internet Top Ten	*http://www.chartshow.co.uk*
Yahoo	*http://dir.yahoo.com/entertainment/ cool_links/index.html*
Cool Site of the Day	*http://www.coolsiteoftheday.com*

1.6 Electric news
1.7 Style check

News sites from Britain, the USA, Canada, Australia, and New Zealand

The Guardian	*http://www.guardian.co.uk*
BBC News	*http://news.bbc.co.uk*
Daily Telegraph	*http://www.telegraph.co.uk*
CNN Interactive	*http://www.cnn.com*
ABC News	*http://www.abcnews.go.com*
The Washington Post	*http://www.washingtonpost.com*
Toronto Globe and Mail	*http://www.globeandmail.com*
Sydney Morning Herald	*http://www.smh.com.au*
Christchurch Press	*http://www.press.co.nz/*

An international list of online newspapers can be found at:

| NewsCentral | *http://www.all-links.com/newscentral/* |

1.8 With a pinch of salt

Sites offering contrasting views on smoking are:

ASH	*http://www.ash.org.uk/*
FORCES	*http://forces.org/*
FOREST	*http://www.forest-on-smoking.org.uk/*

1.9 Lurking detectives

Discussion lists for learners of English can be found at:

| Thomas Robb's Website | *http://www.kyoto-su.ac.jp/~trobb/slinfo.html* |

The lists include discussions on:

INTRO-SL	*Discussion List for New Members (Registered classes only)*
CHAT-SL	*General Discussion List (Low level)*
DISCUSS-SL	*General Discussion List (High level)*
BUSINESS-SL	*Discussion List on Business and Economics*

ENGL-SL	*Discussion List on Learning English*
EVENT-SL	*Discussion List on Current Events*
MOVIE-SL	*Discussion List on the Cinema*
MUSIC-SL	*Discussion List on Music*
SCITECH-SL	*Discussion List on Science, Technology & Computers*
SPORT-SL	*Discussion List on Sports*

Other discussion lists can be found at:

| Dave's ESL Café | *http://www.eslcafe.com/discussion/* |

The format of the messages in these lists is more controlled than in normal discussion lists.

1.10   Electronic holidays

Web addresses where electronic postcards can be found include:

The Electric Postcard	*http://postcards.www.media.mit.edu/ Postcards/*
Blue Mountain	*http://www.bluemountain.com*
Be Mine Greetings	*http://www.bemine.com/*

Some of the cards may include animation and sound, which will require a sound-card. The cards may not work with older versions of Web browsers.

1.11   Post it

Free Web-based discussion lists can be obtained from:

| ListBot | *http://www.listbot.com* |
| Egroups | *http://www.egroups.com* |

1.12   That's telling them

Sites with news discussion features include:

CNN live chat	*http://www.cnn.com/chat/*
CNN message boards	*http://community.cnn.com/*
Lycos message boards	*http://boards.lycos.com/*

2.1   Word treasures

WordNet Lexical Database for English	*http://www.cogsci.princeton.edu/~wn/*
Plumb Design Visual Thesaurus	*http://www.plumbdesign.com/projects/ thesaurus.html*
Roget's Thesaurus	*http://www.thesaurus.com/*
Wordsmyth educational dictionary-thesaurus	*http://www.wordsmyth.net/*

2.2	**Tough questions, cross words**

Quizzes:

Dave Sperling's ESL café	*http://www.pacificnet.net/~sperling/quiz/*
Self-study quizzes for ESL students	*http://www.aitech.ac.jp/~itesls/quizzes/*

Crosswords:

Crossword puzzles for ESL students	*http://www.aitech.ac.jp/~iteslj/cw/*

Anagrams:

Everyday vocabulary anagrams	*http://www.aitech.ac.jp/~itesls/anagrams/*

Exercises and other activities:

Linguistic Funland	*http://www.tesol.net/teslact.html*
Business English Exercises	*http://www.better-english.com/exerciselist .html*
Interactive exercises	*http://www.hut.fi/~rvilmi/LangHelp/ Grammar/#interactive*
Aardvark's EFL Resources	*http://www.english-forum.com/interactive*

2.3	**Everywhere you go, always take the weather with you …**

For information about the current UK weather, go to:

The Met. Office Latest Weather	*http://www.meto.govt.uk/sec3/sec3.html*

Information about international weather can be found at:

The Weather Channel	*http://www.weather.com*
Yahoo! weather	*http://weather.yahoo.com/*
Yellow Pages travel— weather	*http://www.yell.com/travel/weathe/home. html*

Online texts for use in the variation are available at:

Project Gutenberg	*http://www.Gutenberg.net*

2.4	**Holiday essentials**

Lists of international emergency numbers can be found at:

Irish Emergency Ambulance Services	*http://ambulance.ie.eu.org/Numbers.htm*
SOSresponse.Net	*http://www.healthcareland.com/SOS/SO Sresponse.htm*

The emergency numbers for individual countries can be found at:

Rough Guide Travel	*http://travel.roughguides.com*

Currency converters can be found at:

The Universal Currency Converter	*http://www.xe.net/ucc*
Pacific Exchange Rate Service	*http://pacific.commerce.ubc.ca/xr/today.html*
Thomas Cook	*http://www.thomascook.com/*

2.5   **Just the job**

Sites with job information include:

UK Employment service	*http://www.employmentservice.gov.uk/*
Prospects Web	*http://www.prospects.csu.ac.uk/*
Jobs Unlimited	*http://www.jobsunlimited.co.uk*
Top Jobs on the Net	*http://www.topjobs.com/*

2.6   **I do!**

Information about weddings in the UK and USA can be found at:

Weddings.co.uk	*http://www.weddings.co.uk/info/*

2.10   **Consequences**

2.11   **Last question please**

Free Web-based chat rooms can be obtained from:

Beseen	*http://www.beseen.com*
Xoom.com	*http://www.xoom.com/*

3.2   **Valentine's Day**

Love poetry can be found on the following sites:

The Love in Poetry page	*http://www.cc.gatech.edu/grads/b/Gary.N.Boone/beauty_and_love.html*
Poets corner	*http://www.geocities.com/ ~spanoudi/poems/SubjIdx/love.html#table*
Love Poems Weddings.co.uk	*http://www.weddings.co.uk/info/poem.htm*
	http://www.weddings.co.uk/info/poem2.htm

3.3   **The play's the thing**

Free Web-based chat rooms can be obtained from:

Beseen	*http://www.beseen.com*
Xoom.com	*http://www.xoom.com*

3.4   **Alternative school guide**

Informal descriptions of UK educational institutions can be found at:

The Independent's A-Z   *http://www.independent.co.uk/*
  of universities   *advancement/Higher/AZuniversities/*

3.5   **'The Truth is out there'**

The X-Files episode guides   *http://www.thexfiles.com/episodes/*

3.6   **What the critics say**

The following site lists others which accept and publish book reviews:

Where to find book reviews   *http://www1.sympatico.ca/Contents/*
                               Entertainment/literature.html#reviews

For models of book reviews   *http://www.booksunlimited.co.uk*

3.7   **Virtual kitchen**

Resources about health and nutrition can be found at:

Yahoo! health   *http://health.yahoo.com*

The Health Site   *http://www.bbc.co.uk/education/health/*
                               index.shtml

Cyberdiet   *http://www.cyberdiet.com*

Dietitians of Canada   *http://www.dietitians.ca*

(This last is the site upon which the example Food Quiz was based)

3.8   **Step by step**

Websites with instructions of various types are listed here:

Recipes

Don't Cook   *http://www.idontcook.com/*

The Vegetarian Society   *http://www.vegsoc.org/cordonvert/*
                               recipes/index.html

Crafts

The Garden of Origami   *http://ccwf.cc.utexas.edu/~vbeatty/*
                               origami/gate2.html

Great Craft Ideas   *http://www.craftideas.com/ccci/*
                               articleSplash/0,6277,0,00.html
                               Or
                               http://webrequests.com/

Making Web pages

Webmonkey   *http://www.lycos.com/webmonkey/*

Card tricks

The Card Trick Site	*http://www.cardtricks.org.uk/*
The Card Trick Page	*http://hometown.aol.com/chadder424/ ICE-CARDTRICKPAGE.html* Or *http://web.superb.net/cardtric/* for descriptions of tricks

3.9   Academia

Information resources for UK universities include:

UK University and Colleges Service (UCAS)	*http://www.ucas.ac.uk/*
The Independent's A-Z of universities	*http://www.independent.co.uk/ advancement/Higher/AZuniversities/*
Red Mole	*http://www.redmole.co.uk/*

Links to individual universities can be found at:

Red Mole	*http://www.redmole.co.uk/student_mole/ universities.htm*

Information about towns and cities in Britain can be found at:

British Tourist Authority	*http://www.visitbritain.com/*

For information about studying English in the UK, try:

The EFL directory	*http://www.europa-pages.co.uk/uk/*

3.10   Play it again, Sam

Instructions for creating and subscribing to newsgroups can be found at:

All about newsgroups	*http://www.learnthenet.com/english/html/ 26nwsgrp.htm*
Walt's navigating the net forum	*http://www.0.delphi.com/navnet/faq/ newsq.html* Or *http://www.ntlworld.com/help/ newsgroups.htm* Or *http://www.umanitoba.ca/campus/acn/ docs/ns_news.html*

Lists of newsgroups can be found at:

CowTown Hobby newsgroups	*http://www.cowtown.net/hobby.htm*
Deja	*http://www.deja.com/usenet*

The music newsgroup referred to in the example is:

alt.guitar

3.11 Breaking news

RealPlayer, which allows you to play streamed audio and video files on the Internet, can be downloaded free from:

RealNetworks	*http://www.real.com*

Examples of audio news broadcasts can be found at:

Newshour	*http://www.bbc.co.uk/worldservice/ audio_news/newshour.shtml*
CNN audioselect (choose On Demand)	*http://www.cnn.com/audioselect/*

3.12 Audiobooks

Audiobooks can be listened to at:

Broadcast.com AudioBooks	*http://www.broadcast.com/audiobooks/*

3.13 Listen and link

Examples of audio news broadcasts can be found at:

Newshour	*http://www.bbc.co.uk/worldservice/ audio_news/newshour.shtml*
CNN audioselect (choose On Demand)	*http://www.cnn.com/audioselect/*

3.14 Listen and look

To find interesting images, try:

KidsNet Museums Links	*http://www.kidsnet.co.uk/museums.shtml*
Aperture Photo Gallery Archive	*http://www.tssphoto.com/gallery/garchive. html*

Real Audio music clips from CDs can be found at online CD stores, including:

Amazon	*http://www.amazon.com*
Boxman	*http://www.boxma.co.uk/*

(The Interactive Music & Video Shop)

An archive of music in the form of .midi files can be found at:

Daily WAV	*http://www.dailywav.com*

3.15 Fingers crossed

Some sites on the theme of superstitions are:

Superstitions	*http://www.cam.org/~jennyb/super.html*
Superstition: Some common fears and beliefs	*http://www.corsinet.com/trivia/scary.html*

3.16   Knock, knock. Who's there?

Sites with jokes include:

Tower of English Jokes Page	*http://members.tripod.com/ ~towerofenglish/jokes.htm*
Funny.com	*http://www.funny.com*
Humor.com	*http://www.humor.com*

3.17   All in the stars

Fortune-telling sites include:

Astrology and Tarot predictions	*http://www.predictions.net*

3.18   *Desert Island Discs*

Biographies of celebrities can be found at:

The Internet Movie Database	*http://us.imdb.com*
Mr Showbiz	*http://mrshowbiz.go.com/celebrities/index. html*

Real Audio music clips from CDs can be found at online CD stores, including:

Amazon	*http://www.amazon.com*
Boxman	*http://www.boxman.co.uk/*

3.19   Once upon a time

Traditional stories can be found at:

The Online Book Repository	*http://sunsite.org.uk/packages/Online- Book-Initiative/Grimm/*
Cinderella stories (links)	*http://www.acs.ucalgary.ca/~dkbrown/ cinderella.html*
Folk tale links	*http://www.muw.edu/~kdunk/folk.html*

Sources of urban legends include:

The AFU and Urban Legends archive	*http://www.urbanlegends.com*

(AFU = *alt.folklore.urban* newsgroup)

3.20   Salute the flag

Sites with images of national flags include:

Flags of the World	*http://www.emulateme.com/flags/*
Flags of all the states	*http://fotw.digibel.be/flags/iso3166.html*

3.21	**Coming to a theatre near you**

Sites with information about films include:

Movie Review Query Engine	*http://www.mrqe.com*
The Internet Movie Database	*http://us.imdb.com*
Mr. Showbiz	*http://mrshowbiz.go.com/reviews/moviereviews/index.html*

3.22	**Not so automatic**

Free automatic translation can be found at:

Babelfish	*http://babelfish.altavista.com*

3.23	**TranSearch**

The European Union's electronic dictionary for translation is located at:

http://eurodic.ip.lu/cgi-bin/edicbin/EuroDicWWW.pl

3.24	**Cognitive translation**

Listings of international news sources are available at:

NewsCentral	*http://www.all-links.com/newscentral/*
All the World's Newspapers	*http://www.onlinenewspapers.com/*

CNN also reports the news in several languages:

http://www.cnn.com

3.26	**Simultaneous interpreters**

Long audio clips can be found at:

Broadcast.com Audiobooks	*http://www.broadcast.com/audiobooks/*
Newshour	*http://www.bbc.co.uk/worldservice/audio_news/newshour.shtml*

RealPlayer, which allows you to play streamed audio and video files on the Internet, can be downloaded free from:

RealNetworks	*http://www.real.com*

Appendix F Bibliography

Language teaching and learning with the Internet

Eastment, D. 1999. *The Internet and ELT.* London: British Council / Oxford: Summertown.

Gitsake, C. and R. P. Taylor. 1999. *Internet English: WWW-Based Communication Activities.* Oxford: Oxford University Press.

Sperling, D. 1997. *The Internet Guide for English Language Teachers.* Upper Saddle River, N.J.: Prentice Hall Regents.

Sperling, D. 1999. *Dave Sperling's Internet Activity Book.* Upper Saddle River, N.J.: Prentice Hall Regents.

Teeler, D. and P. Gray. 1999. *How to Use the Internet in ELT.* Harlow: Longman.

Warschauer, M. 1995a. *Email for English Teaching: Bringing the Internet and Computer Learning Networks into the Language Classroom.* Alexandria: TESOL.

Warschauer, M. 1995b. *Telecollaboration in Foreign Language Learning.* Hawaii: University of Hawaii Press.

Warschauer, M. 1995c. *Virtual Connections: Online Activities and Projects for Networking Language Learners.* Hawaii: University of Hawaii Press.

Books on language learning and teaching with computers

Boswood, T. (ed.) 1997. *New Ways of Using Computers in Language Teaching.* Alexandria: TESOL.

Healey, D. 1995. *Something to Do on Tuesday.* Houston, Texas: Athelstan Publications.

Levy, M. 1997. *Computer-assisted Language Learning: Context and Conceptualisation.* Oxford: Clarendon Press.

Pennington, M. C. (ed.) 1996. *The Power of CALL.* Houston, Texas: Athelstan.

Books on the Internet and the Web

Crawford, R. and K. Hartley. 1998. *Building a School Web Site.* Cambridge: Pearson Publishing.

Kennedy, A. J. 1998. *Internet: The Rough Guide.* London: Rough Guides.

Kent, P. 1995. *The Complete Idiot's Guide to the World Wide Web.* Indianapolis: Alpha Books.

Levine, J. R. *et al.* 1998. *Internet for Dummies, 5th Edition: The Starter Kit.* Foster City, CA: IDG.

McFedries, P. 1998. *The Complete Idiot's Guide to Creating an HTML Web Page.* Indianapolis: QUE.

Sinclair, I. 1999. *Web Site Construction Simplified.* London: Bernard Babani (Publishing) Ltd.

Tittel, E. and S. N. James. 1998. *HTML 4 For Dummies.* Foster City, CA: IDG.

Young, R. 1997. *The Complete Idiot's Guide to the Internet.* Indianapolis: QUE.

Other titles in the Resource Books for Teachers series

Beginners, by Peter Grundy—communicative activities for both absolute and 'false' beginners, including those who do not know the Roman alphabet. All ages. (ISBN 0 19 437200 6)

Class Readers, by Jean Greenwood—activities to develop extensive and intensive reading skills, plus listening and speaking tasks. All ages. (ISBN 0 19 437103 4)

Classroom Dynamics, by Jill Hadfield—helps teachers maintain a good working relationship with their classes, and so promote effective learning. Teenagers and adults. (ISBN 0 19 437147 6)

Conversation, by Rob Nolasco and Lois Arthur—over 80 activities to develop students' ability to speak confidently and fluently. Teenagers and adults. (ISBN 0 19 437096 8)

Creating Stories with Children, by Andrew Wright—encourages creativity, confidence, and fluency and accuracy in spoken and written English. Age 7–14. (ISBN 0 19 437204 9)

Cultural Awareness, by Barry Tomalin and Susan Stempleski—challenges stereotypes, using cultural issues as a rich resource for language practice. Teenagers and adults. (ISBN 0 19 437194 8)

Dictionaries, by Jonathan Wright—ideas for making more effective use of dictionaries in class. Teenagers and adults. (ISBN 019 437219 7)

Drama, by Charlyn Wessels—creative and enjoyable activities using drama to teach spoken communication skills and literature. Teenagers and adults. (ISBN 0 19 437097 6)

Drama with Children, by Sarah Phillips—practical ideas to develop speaking skills, self-confidence, imagination, and creativity. Age 6–12. (ISBN 0 19 437220 0)

Exam Classes, by Peter May—preparation for a wide variety of public examinations, including most of the main American and British exams. Teenagers and adults. (ISBN 0 19 437208 1)

Games for Children, by Gordon Lewis with Günther Bedson—an exciting collection of games for children aged 4 to 12. (ISBN 0 19 437224 3)

Grammar Dictation, by Ruth Wajnryb—the 'dictogloss' technique—improves understanding and use of grammar by reconstructing texts. Teenagers and adults. (ISBN 0 19 437004 6)

Learner-based Teaching, by Colin Campbell and Hanna Kryszewska—unlocks the wealth of knowledge that learners bring to the classroom. All ages. (ISBN 0 19 437163 8)

Letters, by Nicky Burbidge, Peta Gray, Sheila Levy, and Mario Rinvolucri—using letters and email for language and cultural study. Teenagers and adults. (ISBN 0 19 442149 X)

Listening, by Goodith White—advice and ideas for encouraging learners to become 'active listeners'. Teenagers and adults. (ISBN 0 19 437216 2)

Literature, by Alan Maley and Alan Duff—an innovatory book on using literature for language practice. Teenagers and adults. (ISBN 0 19 437094 1)

Music and Song, by Tim Murphey—'tuning in' to students' musical tastes can increase motivation and tap a rich vein of resources. All ages. (ISBN 0 19 437055 0)

Newspapers, by Peter Grundy—original ideas for making effective use of newspapers in lessons. Teenagers and adults. (ISBN 0 19 437192 6)

Projects with Young Learners, by Diane Phillips, Sarah Burwood, and Helen Dunford—encourages learner independence by producing a real sense of achievement. Age 5 to 13. (ISBN 0 19 437221 9)

Project Work, by Diana L. Fried-Booth—bridges the gap between the classroom and the outside world. Teenagers and adults. (ISBN 0 19 437092 5)

Pronunciation, by Clement Laroy—imaginative activities to build confidence and improve all aspects of pronunciation. All ages. (ISBN 0 19 437087 9)

Role Play, by Gillian Porter Ladousse—controlled conversations to improvised drama, simple dialogues to complex scenarios. Teenagers and adults. (ISBN 0 19 437095 X)

Storytelling with Children, by Andrew Wright—hundreds of exciting ideas for using stories to teach English to children aged 7 to 14. (ISBN 0 19 437202 2)

Translation, by Alan Duff—a wide variety of translation activities from many different subject areas. Teenagers and adults. (ISBN 0 19 437104 2)

Very Young Learners, by Vanessa Reilly and Sheila M. Ward—advice and ideas for teaching children aged 3 to 6 years, including games, songs, drama, stories, and art and crafts. (ISBN 0 19 437209 X)

Vocabulary, by John Morgan and Mario Rinvolucri—a wide variety of communicative activities for teaching new words. Teenagers and adults. (ISBN 019 437091 7)

Writing, by Tricia Hedge—a wide range of writing tasks, as well as guidance on student difficulties with writing. Teenagers and adults. (ISBN 0 19 437098 4)

Young Learners, by Sarah Phillips—advice and ideas for teaching English to children aged 6–12, including arts and crafts, games, stories, poems, and songs. (ISBN 0 19 437195 6)

Index